HILLARY

HILLARY

THE POLITICS
OF PERSONAL
DESTRUCTION

DAVID N. BOSSIE

> ### THE MULTIMEDIA EXPOSÉ:
> ### INCLUDES FULL-LENGTH
> ### DVD DOCUMENTARY

THOMAS NELSON
Since 1798

NASHVILLE DALLAS MEXICO CITY RIO DE JANEIRO BEIJING

Published in Nashville, Tennessee. Thomas Nelson is a registered trademark of Thomas Nelson, Inc.

Thomas Nelson, Inc., titles may be purchased in bulk for educational, business, fund-raising, or sales promotional use. For information, please e-mail SpecialMarkets@ThomasNelson.com.

Library of Congress Cataloging-in-Publication Data

Bossie, David N., 1965-
Hillary : the politics of personal destruction : the companion book to the film "Hillary" now in selected theaters and on DVD / David N. Bossie.
p. cm.
ISBN 978-1-59555-124-5
1. Clinton, Hillary Rodham. 2. Presidents' spouses—United States—Biography. 3. Women legislators—United States—Biography. 4. Women presidential candidates—United States—Biography. 5. United States—Politics and government—2001- 6. United States—Politics and government—1993-2001. 7. United States. Congress. Senate—Biography. I. Title.
E887.C55B67 2008
973.929092—dc22
[B]
2007050779

Printed in the United States of America
08 09 10 11 QW 6 5 4 3 2 1

CONTENTS

INTRODUCTION

On a radio show in 1934, Eleanor Roosevelt was asked, "When will a woman become president?" Her response was simple: when a majority of the American people have trust and confidence in the integrity of that woman.

Has that time arrived?

To find out, we at Citizens United, an organization dedicated to restoring our government to citizens' control, spent the summer of 2007 making a documentary film on Hillary Rodham Clinton—looking at her bid for the presidency from a uniquely personal perspective. Our goal was to peel away the layers of security, tear up the talking points, and get to know the person who today stands across the chasm from the presidency.

Can she leap the chasm?

We interviewed a great many political personalities from both sides of the aisle. We found people who crossed paths with the Clintons—some for better, others not—and we have their stories as never told before. We also visited the city of Clinton, New York, which seemed a fitting place to query constituents of Senator Clinton's. All of these people form the rich fabric of our film, *Hillary The Movie.*

But the film only runs ninety minutes, and our interviews ran nearly one hundred hours and opened up a layered tapestry of insight into this woman who would be president.

We thought we knew Hillary rather well.

But in our interviews we found ourselves amazed time and again as old revelations mixed with new to suggest that this 2008 election will indeed be one for the history books! Our goal, simply, has been to lend insights to the decision you will soon be making—and it is a most profound decision.

From here forward, no punches pulled.

—Dave Bossie

January 2008

MOVIE PARTICIPANTS
(PLUS OTHER SPECIAL COMMENTATORS)

GARY ALDRICH

Senior FBI agent assigned to the White House during the Clinton administration. Appalled by what he saw, he wrote *Unlimited Access: An FBI Agent Inside the Clinton White House* (Regnery, 1998). As with others who found themselves close to the Clintons and duty-bound to warn of their misdeeds, Mr. Aldrich has been reflexively attacked by the liberal media. But in his stories, you'll hear the ominous ring of truth.

DICK ARMEY

House majority leader from 1995 to 2003 and an architect of the Republican Contract with America. In Congress, when Hillary Clinton tried to overhaul healthcare, Mr. Armey recalls her first failure and speculates about HillaryCare II. A former economics professor and an author, Mr. Armey speaks to the pocketbook issues Americans face with an academic's understanding and Texan gumption.

MICHAEL BARONE
Principle coauthor of *The Almanac of American Politics* (National Journal Group, 2007), author of four highly praised books on history and politics, senior writer for *U.S. News and World Report,* and a contributor to FOX News. Mr. Barone is respected for his encyclopedic knowledge of American politics and is regarded as one of the most acute observers of the American political scene.

TONY BLANKLEY
Until recently the editorial page editor of the *Washington Times,* and co-host of public radio's *Left, Right & Center,* as well as author of *The West's Last Chance: Will We Win the Clash of Civilizations?* (Regnery 2006) Mr. Blankley was previously House Speaker Gingrich's press secretary and President Reagan's policy analyst and speechwriter. Mr. Blankley's assessment of Mrs. Clinton's record includes an intriguing comparison with Richard M. Nixon.

MARSHALL BROWN
A farmer in Smyrna, New York, and a constituent of Senator Clinton's.

BAY BUCHANAN
Author of *The Extreme Makeover of Hillary (Rodham) Clinton* and youngest ever treasurer of the United States, appointed by President Reagan. A frequent commentator on television, she is often asked about the "new" Hillary and offers an intimate look at the "makeover."

DAN BURTON
As a thirteen-term congressman serving Indiana's Fifth Congressional District, Mr. Burton was chairman of the Government Reform and Oversight Committee that investigated the endless stream of abuses and illegalities committed by the Clintons. He explains how Hillary escaped indictment once and wonders whether she will again.

AMANDA CARPENTER

Author of *The Vast Right-Wing Conspiracy's Dossier on Hillary Clinton* (Regnery, 2006). As a Washington reporter who has seen Hillary up close, and as a part of the "young woman demographic" Hillary is counting on for victory, Ms. Carpenter is a prism through which Hillary's appeal is more clearly viewed.

JOE CONNOR

The Connor family has been touched twice by terrorism—first in 1975 when FALN terrorists murdered Frank Connor, and again in 2001 when al-Qaeda terrorists murdered Steve Schlag, a cousin. Joe Connor tells the story Hillary doesn't want you to hear—about how the Clintons reopened the wounds of the Connor family, merely for political gain.

ANN COULTER

A six-time best-selling author, including her latest: *If Democrats Had Any Brains They'd Be Republicans* (Crown Forum, 2007). Coulter is a nationally syndicated columnist and also the author of *High Crimes and Misdemeanors: The Case Against Bill Clinton* (Regnery, 2002).

BILLY DALE

The former director of the White House Travel Office, Mr. Dale's story is possibly the most tragic of the Clinton years. His account is a firsthand testament to Hillary Clinton's ruthlessness.

MITCH FREEMAN

Dr. Freeman practices medicine in Yuma, Arizona, and offers a frontline view of the price of Hillary's healthcare plans. Born in Iraq, Dr. Freeman has strong thoughts about the current war in Iraq as well.

JOHN FUND

Longtime writer for the *Wall Street Journal* editorial section and author most recently of *Stealing Elections: How Voter Fraud Threatens Our Democracy* (Encounter Books, 2004).

FRANK GAFFNEY

An author of *War Footing: 10 Steps America Must Take to Prevail in the War for the Free World* (Naval Institute Press, 2005) and the deputy assistant secretary of defense under President Reagan. Mr. Gaffney offers perspective on past efforts to fight terrorism and Hillary's qualifications for fighting for our future.

JEFF GERTH

Coauthor of *Her Way: The Hopes and Ambitions of Hillary Rodham Clinton* (Little, Brown, and Company, 2007). A *New York Times* reporter for more than a quarter century, he won a Pulitzer for reporting on the corporate sale of secret technology to China. He also broke the Whitewater story.

NEWT GINGRICH

Elected Speaker of the House in 1994, Mr. Gingrich was a principal architect of the Contract with America. He has since authored nine books including *Saving Lives & Saving Money* (Alexis de Tocqueville Institution, 2006)—outlining a sensible healthcare plan for America. Mr. Gingrich knows Hillary's old healthcare plan and the economic policies we could expect if she is elected.

RICK HAHN

Now a retired FBI agent, Mr. Hahn was part of the FBI team that mobilized to track down the Puerto Rican FALN terrorists after they struck New York City in 1975. He knows firsthand the terrible price we're paying today for the Clintons' politicizing of terrorism in days past.

BOB HASENOEHRL

Owner of a trucking company in western New York and a constituent of Senator Clinton's.

LEE HIEB

Dr. Hieb is an orthopedic spine surgeon in Yuma, Arizona, and she offers a frontline view of the price we would pay for Hillary's healthcare plans.

EDWARD KLEIN

Author of *The Truth About Hillary: What She Knew, When She Knew It, and How Far She'll Go to Become President* (Sentinel Trade, 2006), Mr. Klein has been more viciously attacked by the Clinton political machine than perhaps any other, because he has dug deep into the "personal life" of Hillary and shared a less flattering portrait than we were meant to see. Yet since she wants to be our president, shouldn't we see all we're getting into?

LARRY KUDLOW

Host of CNBC's *Kudlow and Company*, contributor to *National Review*, author of *American Abundance: The New Economic and Moral Prosperity* (Harper Collins, 1997), and associate director of the Office of Management and Budget under President Reagan. Mr. Kudlow makes a strong case for grabbing on to your pocketbook if Hillary is elected.

MICHAEL LEDEEN

A Freedom Scholar with the American Enterprise Institute and author of many books including *The Iranian Time Bomb: The Mullah Zealots Quest for Destruction* (Truman Talley Books, 2007) and *The War Against The Terror Masters: Why It Happened. Where We Are Now. How We'll Win.* (St. Martin's Griffin, 2003). His warnings about the dire threats the next president will face give pause to every American headed to the voting booth.

Mark Levin

A nationally popular radio talk show host, best-selling author, former chief of staff to Attorney General Ed Meese, and president of the Landmark Legal Foundation, Mr. Levin is one of conservatism's leading proselytizers. His radio show has been rated number one in its time slot in New York, Chicago, Detroit, Dallas, and Washington, D.C.

Keith Lewicki

A small businessman in Smyrna, New York, and a constituent of Senator Clinton's.

Clare Lopez

Spent twenty years as a field operative for the CIA, working both domestically and abroad in Central/South America, Africa, and the Balkans to collect information related to our national security. She has experienced firsthand the effects of the Clinton budget cuts on our nation's military and security forces.

Charlie Luberger

A farmer in Smyrna, New York, and a constituent of Senator Clinton's.

George Marlin

George Marlin is the former executive director of the Port Authority of New York and New Jersey. Mr. Marlin shows how Hillary's approach to governance has failed New York, and how, if elected president, it could impact people in other states.

Angela McGlowan

As the author of *Bamboozled: How Americans Are Being Exploited by the Lies of the Liberal Agenda* (Thomas Nelson, 2007) and a FOX News analyst, she speaks with refreshing candor about Hillary's pandering to minorities to gain their votes and then reveals what Hillary actually delivers once in office.

MICHAEL MEDVED

A nationally syndicated radio host, best-selling author, and film critic. His tenth book, *Right Turns: From Liberal Activist to Conservative Champion in 35 Unconventional Lessons* (Three Rivers Press, 2005), chronicles his dramatic transition from "punk liberal activist" to "lovable conservative curmudgeon." No public figure (who will talk publicly) has known Hillary Clinton longer, or better.

JOHN MICA

As an eight-term congressman serving Florida's 7th District, Mr. Mica is a senior member of the Government Oversight and Reform Committee that investigated the endless stream of abuses and illegalities committed by the Clintons and their allies.

RICHARD MINITER

Author of *Losing bin Laden: How Bill Clinton's Failures Unleashed Global Terror* (Regnery, 2004) and *Shadow War: The Untold Story of How Bush is Winning the War on Terror* (Regnery, 2005) and editorial page writer for the *Wall Street Journal Europe*, Mr. Miniter has appeared on numerous TV and radio programs to assess the impact of terrorism on our country to date. He now explains precisely why Hillary is not equipped to convincingly fight the war on terror as it transitions to the next stage.

MICHAEL MORRILL

A small businessman in Smyrna, New York, and a constituent of Senator Clinton's.

DICK MORRIS

Called "the most influential private citizen in America" by *Time*, Mr. Morris has known Bill and Hillary since 1977 and has directed a number of their campaigns. He has authored several books including *Rewriting History* (Harper, 2005), a refutation of Hillary's biography *Living History*, and *Condi vs. Hillary: The Next Great Presidential Race* (Harper, 2006). For those who have had enough of the old Clinton scandals, Mr. Morris has uncovered new scandals Hillary will have to hurdle to win the presidency.

BOB NOVAK

A political commentator known for writing *Inside Report* since 1963 and hosting TV news shows including *The Capital Gang* and *Crossfire*. His book *The Prince of Darkness: 50 Years Reporting in Washington* (Crown Forum, 2007) chronicles fifty years of reporting in Washington. Few people bring more perspective than Mr. Novak to the long sweep of politics, and what will happen if Hillary is included in that sweep.

CYRUS NOWRASTEH

An accomplished filmmaker, having written and directed *The Day Reagan Was Shot* and TV shows including *La Femme Nikita, DEA,* and *Falcon Crest*. His miniseries *The Path to 9/11* aired on ABC in September 2006 and was a huge ratings smash despite a vicious, Bill Clinton-directed campaign to censor the movie. Now the Clintons are succeeding in squelching the DVD release of his movie, and Nowrasteh explains why.

KATE O'BEIRNE

Author of *Women Who Make the World Worse: and How Their Radical Feminist Assault Is Ruining Our Schools, Families, Military, and Sports* (Sentinel, 2005), Washington editor for *National Review*, member of *The Capital Gang,* and a former deputy assistant secretary of the Department of Health and Human Services, under President Reagan. In showing how Hillary has corroded feminism, we see how that corrosion would continue if Hillary wins.

JIM PARKER

A farmer in Smyrna, New York, and a constituent of Senator Clinton's.

BUZZ PATTERSON

Lieutenant Colonel Patterson was President Clinton's senior military aid, responsible for carrying the "nuclear football." What he experienced drove him to write *Dereliction of Duty: The Eyewitness Account of How Bill Clinton Compromised America's National Security* (Regnery, 2004). His stories about the dangers both Bill and Hillary Clinton placed this nation into are at once harrowing and instructive for the electoral choices ahead.

PETER PAUL

A twice-convicted felon with a remarkable past that includes his becoming the biggest fund-raiser for Hillary Clinton. The seduction and betrayal of Peter Paul offers a cautionary tale for the management style Hillary Clinton would bring to the presidency.

JARED STERN

A private investigator hired by friends of the Clintons to threaten and intimidate Kathleen Willey.

AARON TONKEN

Currently in federal prison, he pleaded guilty in December 2003 on mail and wire fraud involving the finances of charities. Tonken was Hillary's closest friend in Hollywood and, as he wrote in *King of Cons: Exposing the Dirty, Rotten Secrets of the Washington Elite and Hollywood*

Celebrities (Thomas Nelson, 2004), responsible for hooking up the Clintons with celebrities and hosting big illegal fund-raisers.

R. EMMETT TYRRELL

Founder and editor in chief of the *American Spectator* magazine, adjunct fellow at the Hudson Institute, and contributing editor of the *New York Sun*, Mr. Tyrrell is one of the nation's foremost experts on all things Clinton. He is the author of numerous books, most recently 2003's *Madame Hillary: The Dark Road to the White House* (Regnery), and 2007's *The Clinton Crack-Up: The Boy President's Life After the White House* (Thomas Nelson).

KATHLEEN WILLEY

She began the 1980s as one of the Clintons' most devoted supporters—then Bill Clinton cornered her and both Clintons turned their politics of personal destruction on her.

HILLARY'S RUNNING FOR PRESIDENT, BUT SHOULD SHE BE FACING INDICTMENT?

When it comes to the shady business of campaign fund-raising, Hillary Clinton's modus operandi has always been to raise as much cash as possible, regardless of the veracity of the source. In 1992, it was James Riady. In 1996, it was Johnny Chung. In 2000, it was Peter Paul.

There are some who lead oversized lives, pursuing great dreams and extraordinary enterprises while all too often skirting the law. Peter Paul is such a man. One of his more dubious achievements was becoming the biggest fund-raiser for Hillary Clinton's 2000 Senate bid and unleashing the most spectacular campaign spending fraud in U.S. history.

PETER PAUL'S COLLISION COURSE WITH HILLARY CLINTON

We spoke with Peter Paul in his home in North Carolina where he was awaiting sentencing on a second felony conviction. We asked right from the start why people should believe his version of events:

I don't expect anybody to take what I say at face value. I ask people to look at the public record. Look at [Hillary Clinton's] responses to my legal pleadings. Look at her sworn declarations, and look at mine. Look at testimony of friends of Hillary's who testified about the corruption in her campaign. It corroborates all that I'm about to tell you.

The seeds for Paul's collision course with Hillary Clinton were planted in Miami in the 1970s, years before he met her:

I set a goal for myself to transform sleepy little Miami into an international trade center. One of my projects was the development of the World Trade Center in Miami. I wanted to make a mark on my hometown with this project. So I hired the foremost architect in the country, I. M. Pei. I got the air rights to build *over* the convention center—this was a first in using air rights. And I got the Department of Commerce to grant a license to own and operate the largest foreign trade zone in the United States.

In the course of this enterprise, I ended up representing political figures and foreign governments in the region. And I began collecting people as friends and clients. First into my collection was the artist Salvador Dali. We became friends quickly because we could converse; he would start in French, Spanish, or English and go through a series of languages until he got to the end of the sentence. I also represented Andy Warhol and worked with Peter Max, but my focus was on international trade.

Fidel Castro had been trying to undermine democracies in the region. So I began representing anti-Castro leaders, and I directed a sting on Castro to reveal how he was buying black market coffee and selling it to the Russians as "Cuban coffee" and personally pocketing the difference. We succeeded in depriving Castro of close to $9 million.

Unfortunately, Jimmy Carter was president, and he decided to use our activities to enhance his relations with Castro. Rather than enforce the Trading with the Enemy Act, Carter secretly helped Castro recover the money I took from him. This led me to work undercover with various task forces to reveal that, in fact, Carter—through his finance manager, Burt Lance—had a secret relationship with Castro in which they actually laundered Castro's drug money into Carter's presidential campaign.

At the end of it all, I pleaded guilty to a felony count of conspiring to defraud the Cuban government and possession of cocaine. I was sentenced to eight years, reduced to five-and-a-half years when agents from three U.S. agencies explained the extenuating circumstances to the judge.

In the next chapter of my life, with the help of Reagan's kitchen cabinet in California, I became associated with some Hollywood icons and I began publishing biographies of celebrities including Buzz Aldrin, Tony Curtis, and Muhammad Ali. Jimmy Stewart and I started a foundation to help emerging democracies behind the former Iron Curtain. On the first Christmas after the breakup of the Soviet Union, I directed the broadcast of *It's a Wonderful Life* to 200 million Russians who had never seen an American production. It was glorious!

Next I wanted to prove I could turn an out-of-work model into a media icon. So here was this fellow Fabio Lanzoni; he wanted to be a Van Damme or a Schwarzenegger, but was getting nowhere. I helped him understand that he had a constituency of 28 million romance readers who didn't know he was a real person. So I got the top literary agent in the business to represent Fabio as an author. Now, Fabio didn't speak English very well, and he didn't write very well. But we overcame that and got the biggest advance for a romance book ever—$100,000. Fabio became the first *male* romance writer, and within eighteen months I had him on the cover of *People* magazine.

That led me to Hillary for the first time. I arranged a book signing for Fabio in the White House. I wanted a photo that would top the one Nancy Reagan had taken with Mr. T. I figured that if I could get Fabio to lift Hillary up into a romance pose, that would top them all. So I got a private meeting with the Clintons, Danny DeVito, and Fabio. And at one point, I induced the men to chase Hillary around the table. She was in a ball gown, and she was concerned about being too heavy for Fabio to pick her up gracefully. She ultimately just sat down on the floor to stop things. Bill Clinton told her not to be a prude. And Fabio reached down, lifted the First Lady up by her posterior, and coaxed her into taking photos. I sent Hillary roses many times after that!

Next time I saw Hillary, she was beginning her campaign for the Senate. I reminded her of that encounter and asked for a copy of the Hillary-Fabio photo from the official White House photographer. She said that if I helped her campaign, she could get that photo for me.

Meanwhile, I had become a business partner with Stan Lee, the creator of Spider-Man. We wanted to export inspirational stories to kids around the world who were in desperate need of inspiration. It dawned on me that if I could hire an ex-president to help us in Asia and Europe, we could accomplish our objective within the lifetime of my partner—who was seventy-nine. So I embarked on an effort to hire Bill Clinton when he left the White House as a rainmaker for our company, Stan Lee Media.

At this time, an old employee of mine, Aaron Tonken, came to see me. He had, through Denise Rich, befriended the Gores and the Clintons and helped them in their Hollywood fund-raising activities. Aaron needed my help in building up his importance in the eyes of his political contacts. If I would help him, he would help me attain my business objectives.

AARON TONKEN HELPS HILLARY IN HOLLYWOOD

Aaron Tonken is currently an inmate at Ashland Federal Correctional Institution in Kentucky. He was sentenced in August 2004 to sixty-three months in prison for pleading guilty to one count of mail fraud and one count of wire fraud for the mishandling of monies to charities. He was taking money meant for one charity and putting it into other charities. Like Peter Paul, there is a rather colorful story behind Aaron Tonken:

> In the early 1990s, I was living in a homeless shelter. One day I met Zsa Zsa Gabor and ended up moving into her Bel-Air estate as her assistant. In that capacity I met all of Hollywood very quickly. My overall impression of celebrities and entertainment executives was not a good one. I found them to be consumed with greed, self-indulgence, pride, and arrogance.
>
> Through Zsa Zsa I met Peter Paul. He gave me an office and his Rolodex, and I would basically call all the relationships Peter Paul had. I would get to know these name celebrities—people like Charlton Heston, Milton Berle, Ed McMahon—and spend time talking to them and convincing them to attend parties.
>
> One day my friend and client Natalie Cole invited me to a lunch with President and Mrs. Clinton. At the last minute, I was required to pay $50,000 to come, so I wrote the check. Once the Clintons found that I had access to celebrities, they hungrily pursued me.
>
> I found Mrs. Clinton to be very engaging. When she speaks to you, you're the only person in the room. She's very warm, very interested in what you have to say. My relationship with Mrs. Clinton was much closer than with Mr. Clinton. She would call me, let me ride in the car on campaign trips, visit movie sets with me, allow me to visit the White House often.
>
> In various videos Mrs. Clinton has made for me, she has referred

to "my good friend, Aaron Tonken" and told a roomful of supporters that "she's fortunate to have made me as a friend." We had a growing relationship, though I don't know where it ultimately would have led, since most everyone who gets close to the Clintons winds up in prison.

Aaron Tonken's first big project with Peter Paul in February 2000 was to cohost a fund-raiser with Bill Clinton and the governor of California. Peter Paul was clear on his own objectives in hosting this event:

I paid $30,000 for this event, and I told Aaron I wanted a video clip of Bill Clinton talking about Stan Lee's superheroes. But the evening wore down and Bill Clinton was leaving, and still no video clip. I repeated to Aaron that I really needed that clip. So Aaron planted himself in front of the president and his Secret Service contingent and turned the president on his heels and forced him to come back and give me the message I wanted. When I saw that Aaron was able to do that, I believed he could help me reach the president with an offer.

At this event, I was introduced to the chairman of the Democratic Party, Ed Rendell, and I asked his advice in hiring the president. He said that if I gave $500,000, I would be among the top five contributors to the party and therefore would be able to spend quality time with the president.

Ed Rendell and I talked again soon after that, and this time he suggested that since Hillary's campaign was heating up, I should become a donor to her campaign.

Why were Hillary and Bill Clinton, and Democratic Party leaders, working in earnest with a man like Peter Paul?

When I began planning fund-raisers for the Clintons, I was required to give my Social Security number, birth date, and so forth. I was worried that they'd find my convictions from the 1970s objectionable. But I passed muster. From then on, they had all the details about my past.

Aaron Tonken was much closer to Hillary than Peter Paul was, and he offers another view on Hillary's feelings about her new largest fundraiser:

> Peter Paul was basically paying for these fund-raising events for Hillary, but he was kept at arm's length. I had been invited fourteen times to the White House. Peter Paul hadn't been invited even once. Hillary didn't speak with him except when I forced it. So she definitely did business with him but kept a certain distance so she could disassociate from him quickly if need be.

Hillary did plenty of "business" with Peter Paul, with Aaron Tonken serving as a convenient middleman. In return for $150,000 plus event costs, Peter Paul was permitted to host a luncheon at Spago for influential denizens of Hollywood.

Aaron Tonken recalls the Spago luncheon:

> I told Hillary that I would raise millions for her if she would have lunch with me at Spago. When celebrities saw me with politicians, they would think me important. When politicians saw me with celebrities, they would think me important. So we lunched at Spago. I paid Dionne Warwick $10,000 to sing "That's What Friends Are For." I invited some deep Democratic pockets, along with Mrs. Larry King, Olivia Newton-John, and the wife of Wolfgang Puck. It was all very showy.
>
> At the time I was completely ignorant of the Federal Election Commission or any of the laws regarding political fund-raising. So I didn't even know the dangers I was wading into.

Seated next to Hillary at the luncheon, Peter Paul recalls delving into legally gray areas:

I was testing the waters with Hillary to see how far I could go into my colorful career. But she was unfazed by it all. We talked about my experiences as an international lawyer, my anti-Castro activities, and my investigation of Burt Lance.

In the course of sharing our "pasts" during the bonding session we had during a VIP lunch I hosted for her at Spago in Beverly Hills, June 9, 2000, I made references to my swashbuckling days as an international lawyer in Miami in the 1970s when I led a plot to expose Fidel Castro's frauds on his benefactors in the Soviet union while liberating almost $10 million from his personal piggy bank, the Banco Nacional de Cuba. These activities, during Jimmy Carter and Bert Lance's control of the government, resulted in my receiving two felony convictions and a suspension of my law license, which clearly did not bother her. (See my latest court filing in *Paul v. Clinton et al.*)

She did discuss fate and destiny with me and her belief that we are all predestined to the lives we live. She intimated her conviction that her destiny could lead her to becoming the most reknown [sic] woman in history, and I had the distinct impression it was based on her presumption of a career beyond being the first copresident of the U.S. and the first First Lady to become a U.S. senator. Hillary's announcement is clearly not a surprise to anyone who has known and followed Hillary's career—it was in fact anticlimactic in the controlled, low key way she threw her considerable girth into the ring. But the notion that she is interested in a conversation with her fellow Americans signals the beginning of the most cynical, Clinton-speak propaganda campaign since

Joseph Goebbels and Lenni Riefenstahl got together to develop a winning political campaign for Mr. Shickelgruber. The American people, and America as we know, it is now "officially" threatened by the greatest internal political threat that has ever confronted our civil liberties and our constitutional democracy. (http://www.peterfpaul.com/2007/01/)

I was a little nervous, because I had my video camera on—and I wanted to lead her into a gray area. The president cannot sign contracts when he's in the White House, but he certainly can negotiate a deal so that when he leaves the White House, he's ready to sign. But I had nothing to worry about—Hillary said she would help in any way she could.

Turns out, we had something in common: the winter carnival years before at Dartmouth. Hillary had been set up on a blind date for the carnival with a fellow I knew from California. He was a surfer and wasn't happy in the snows of New Hampshire, so he proceeded to get drunk and abandon her. He was so drunk, she recalled, that he took his surf board and tried to surf the hills of a golf course. She had quite a vivid recollection.

Hillary could quickly remember the blind date, the roses, those kinds of things. But in testimony under oath as First Lady, she said, "I don't know" or "I don't remember" a record two hundred and fifty times. Peter Paul gave us additional insight into her selective memory:

She can't remember significant details of things that happened a few months prior, yet she has detailed recollections of things that happened twenty and thirty years earlier. Talk to her today and she doesn't have much recollection of the interactions we had at this critical moment in her life. She doesn't remember inducing me to be her biggest donor. She doesn't remember that I was her donor at all.

What's interesting is she has not denied any of the allegations I have made. I filed a sworn declaration, which laid out all our conversations in great detail. Her response was not that I'm a liar and not that I didn't do what I said. Her response under oath was she "doesn't remember the conversations, and if we had those conversations [she] would remember, so therefore we couldn't have had the conversations." That's a clever non-denial denial.

After the Spago event, Peter Paul sought and received additional assurances from the Clintons that they were ready to become business partners. So he dispatched Aaron Tonken to a Chicago fund-raiser to begin planning a big fund-raiser for Hillary:

At the Chicago fund-raiser, Hillary's finance director, David Rosen, and personal assistant, Kelly Craighead, introduced me to Jim Levin— a close friend of the president who would keep an eye on things. And we all went out afterward to a nightclub. I remember it was raining that night, and Jim ran out quickly to his car. It was brand-new, the most expensive Mercedes you could buy. I commented on its beauty. Kelly Craighead turned and said, "His cars get repossessed every three to six months." I didn't yet know that this close friend of the Clintons not only owned strip clubs in Chicago but was under investigation and ultimately indicted for extortion and fraud.

At the nightclub that night, we hatched a plan to hold a big gala in just eight weeks. It would be a final Hollywood tribute to the president, and a fund-raiser for Mrs. Clinton's Senate campaign.

Afterward, Jim Levin went to Camp David to convince the president to participate. Kelly Craighead worked on her end with her boss, Mrs. Clinton. I convinced Peter Paul to put up half the money. Hillary's finance director, David Rosen, basically moved into our offices and began working the donors. And I began putting the event together.

DEFTLY ENGINEERING THE BIGGEST CAMPAIGN FINANCE FRAUD

It was an ambitious goal—to organize a major fund-raiser in just a few weeks. But Peter Paul was more than up to the task:

We talked about a budget of $1.1 million, and I agreed to pay half. I was responsible for the guest list, the seating, the invitations. I was willing to write the checks necessary to accomplish what would otherwise have been impossible—a major star-studded event from concept to production in a few weeks. But I could only do it if the president cooperated. And he did.

At the time, I was also busy building Stan Lee Media. I had a lot on my plate! So I delegated the bill-paying for the gala to a controller. He managed all the accounts—so I never knew exactly how much I was spending. And I actually took a five-day vacation in the middle of this with my family—I had promised them! When I returned on August 4, I was told that we had already spent $1.3 million. I got furious and almost physically assaulted Hillary's finance director, David Rosen, because of the cost escalation that I had not agreed to.

At the time the *Los Angeles Times* (Richard B. Schmitt, "Inquiry Focuses on Hillary Clinton Campaigner," 13 December 2003) reported that David Rosen effectively coerced Peter Paul into continuing to fund the gala by telling him Hillary would cancel the event and blame it all on him if he didn't keep paying all the bills.

Equally important, Peter Paul's expenses were defined by federal election law as contributions to Hillary's election campaign, and she was required to report them to the Federal Elections Commission. Did she? No, according to Peter Paul.

> David Rosen basically said he didn't want to hear about the costs. Whatever they were, he didn't want to hear about them. At one point he just covered his ears and ran from the room.
>
> All of the expenses I paid for various fund-raisers for Hillary were never *legally* reported. Either they weren't reported at all, or they were reported as originating from other individuals, and the full amount was not reported.

Aaron Tonken confirms that the man who was supposed to be handling finances for Hillary was out to lunch:

> I remember in the lobby of the St. Regis Hotel in Beverly Hills telling David Rosen what was happening. His direct answer was, "I'm just going to pretend I don't know, if they ask me."

Election campaign law can be rather complex, and the lawyers for candidates spend a lot of time trying to sort it all out. Some of them find a way to skirt it, says Peter Paul:

> Good lawyers, like Hillary and their team, find ways to skirt the law and make sure they don't get caught.
>
> When I finally saw the finance reports that Hillary's campaign had filed with the Federal Elections Commission in February 2001, I discovered that they had reported only a small amount of the actual expenditures I made on their behalf. I was quite surprised and did not want to be a coconspirator with them in breaking the law. So I went to the U.S. Attorney's office and explained what had happened.

Under federal law, if a candidate or a candidate's agent is involved in soliciting or coordinating an expenditure by a supporter, that expenditure is considered a donation to the campaign. Even if the money is paid to a third party, such as in incurring expenses for a fund-raising event, it is considered an "in-kind" contribution. It's known as a "hard money" contribution, and there are limits to the amount you can give. As a candidate, you are not allowed to reallocate those contributions to any other committees (what we've come to know as "soft money") to avoid the limitations.

Peter Paul says that although he was an attorney, he knew little about federal election law:

> I wasn't aware of the relevant Federal Election Commission laws. But I discovered that even if Hillary was involved only indirectly through Kelly Craighead in conceiving the event, soliciting money to pay for the event, and coordinating expenditures for the event, both of them were violating federal law.
>
> There was never any doubt about the extent of my efforts on her behalf. In a phone call I had with her—a call I videotaped [discussed later]—she said she understood how difficult these things could be, especially with so little time to prepare. She made it clear that she was being briefed on a daily basis.

Aaron Tonken remembers Hillary's involvement quite vividly:

> It was in July when Hillary Clinton called the offices of Stan Lee Media. David Rosen took the call. I was there with Peter Paul and Stan Lee. She thanked Peter for all he was doing; she said that she had spoken to Kelly Craighead and had been debriefed on all that was happening with the event.

Hillary's claim under oath that she "had no knowledge of the financial dealings" begins to fall apart when Paul relates the details of the event planning:

> Early on, Hillary demanded that I hire a friend of hers, a CBS producer by the name of Gary Smith, to produce the gala. I had wanted to use my friend Dick Clark. But because of Hillary's demands, Gary Smith became the biggest vendor of the gala. Hillary negotiated his fee for services—it was an exorbitant $800,000. When I complained, Hillary negotiated the fee down $50,000. Then the night before the gala, Smith demanded an additional $75,000, and when I complained again, I was told I had to go along with it. All this is important because it offers irrefutable evidence that Hillary was involved in the planning of the event that she claims to have little or no memory of.

Aaron Tonken has a somewhat different recollection of the role Hillary played in the planning of the August 12 gala, though he reaches similar conclusions:

> Originally, Peter Paul was looking to have Dick Clark Productions put on the gala, but it was too pricey. I had wanted to work with Gary Smith—he had produced the Emmys, the Grammys, the Democratic National Convention. I outlined our vision to him and then he put together a budget and fees for Peter Paul, along with a request for a substantial deposit. Peter Paul wasn't happy with the fees. So he spoke with David Rosen, who must have then spoken with Hillary Clinton. We know this for two reasons:
> One, Gary Smith admitted to receiving a call from Mrs. Clinton regarding the fees. And two, Gary Smith came back with a lower fee. Now in her affidavit in the Peter Paul civil suit, Hillary states that she

didn't negotiate the fees or know about the fees of Gary Smith. But that was simply impossible, given what we know.

Anyone who gazed out upon the 125-acre estate of Ken Roberts on Mandeville Canyon Road in Brentwood, California, that night of August 12 bore witness to one of the biggest fund-raising scandals in history. Peter Paul was proud of what they had accomplished so quickly, but was also nervous:

> This was the biggest fund-raising event ever produced. We had my friends Mohammed Ali, John Travolta, Brad Pitt, Shirley MacLaine, the Steenburgens, and Gregory Peck. We had headliners Cher, Diana Ross, Patty LaBelle, Toni Braxton, Melissa Etheridge, Sugar Ray, Michael Bolton, and Paul Anka.
>
> There was a stage equal to the Grammy Awards with over one hundred movie stars, eight big international headliners, most of the big names in Hollywood, the entire leadership of the Democratic Party. And the emotions that were invoked, and the nostalgia for the Clinton years, made it a truly magical evening out under the stars. Everyone said that it was the most extraordinary evening they had ever spent.
>
> As a fund-raiser, all attendees were supposed to be contributors. But I had hired or incentivized many celebrities to appear. I figured their appearance would make it look like they were endorsing Hillary's candidacy—whether they were or not. It was a big PR coup for Hillary and invaluable to her campaign because she was at the time locked in a neck-and-neck race for the New York seat.
>
> The fact that all of these violations occurred in plain view of the media, Hollywood, and the Democratic Party is extraordinary. The further fact that these violations were covered up, and that federal

investigations into these violations were obstructed by allies of the Clintons, is even more extraordinary.

Aaron Tonken was proud of the event, despite all the hassles of marrying Hollywood and Washington talent:

Almost all of the performers made crazy demands—typical of self-indulgent Hollywood. People don't realize how temperamental and demanding and abusive John Travolta is, for example. His publicist at Rogers & Cowan, Paul Block, said that Travolta would not partici-pate in the evening unless he could make a toast separate from other entertainers at the dinner. No one else, civilian or celebrity, could make the toast. He had to be the only one. That was his first condi-tion. His second condition was that he sit right next to the president. He was a huge pain, but we put up with his demands because we wanted him there.

Because of Travolta, we had to move Brad Pitt and Jennifer Aniston, who were both bigger than all the other stars, to Mrs. Clinton's table. Most of the stars didn't want to sit with Mrs. Clinton. They all wanted to sit with the president.

Cher had never met the Clintons. Never voted for Bill Clinton. She had to be paid under the table. She also insisted that her makeup artist be flown in first-class from New York and be allowed to do Hillary's makeup! It took some wrangling, but Mrs. Clinton agreed to have her makeup removed before she arrived at the event and then to have it reapplied by Cher's person. As it turned out, when Mrs. Clinton arrived at the event you could see she was exhausted, and her staff surrounded me and asked, "Please, does she still have to do this?" And I was embarrassed, really, to push it, so I canceled it. Cher was very mad, as was her makeup artist—but it was a ridiculous demand.

WHEN PEOPLE STARTED ASKING QUESTIONS, HILLARY HID

After the event, the media began asking questions. Were campaign laws being broken, as it appeared? And who was this mysterious Peter Paul? Paul recalls:

I got a phone call from Ed Rendell saying the *Washington Post* was asking questions about my past, and Hillary was taking the position that she hardly knew me, and that I didn't give her any money. Rendell also made it abundantly clear that if I was smart and wanted to keep my deal, I would go along with the deceit. So I was induced to join them in lying to the public, which I regret and apologize for. But after spending nearly $2 million, I just wasn't ready to walk away because the *Washington Post* happened to be writing a story.

When reporters discovered that I had in fact contributed the maximum allowable $2,000, Hillary's spokesperson two-stepped and said they were refunding the money that same day, and that they wouldn't take any more money from me.

Then in another article, Hillary's spokesman, Howard Wolfson, finally admitted that the gala cost over $1 million but claimed it was a legal in-kind contribution. Those assertions were false, obviously so. But I didn't make an issue of it because I didn't want to jeopardize any chance I still had to make a deal with Bill Clinton.

While publicly distancing herself from me, Hillary was privately writing me glowing letters of thanks (see Figure 1). Her letters indicated to me that our relationship was in good standing.

I was also being reassured privately by Ed Rendell to just sit tight until the Clintons left the White House. Then everything would come together.

So I asked the Clintons to show me some love by allowing my partner, Mr. Oto, to attend one final dinner at the White House

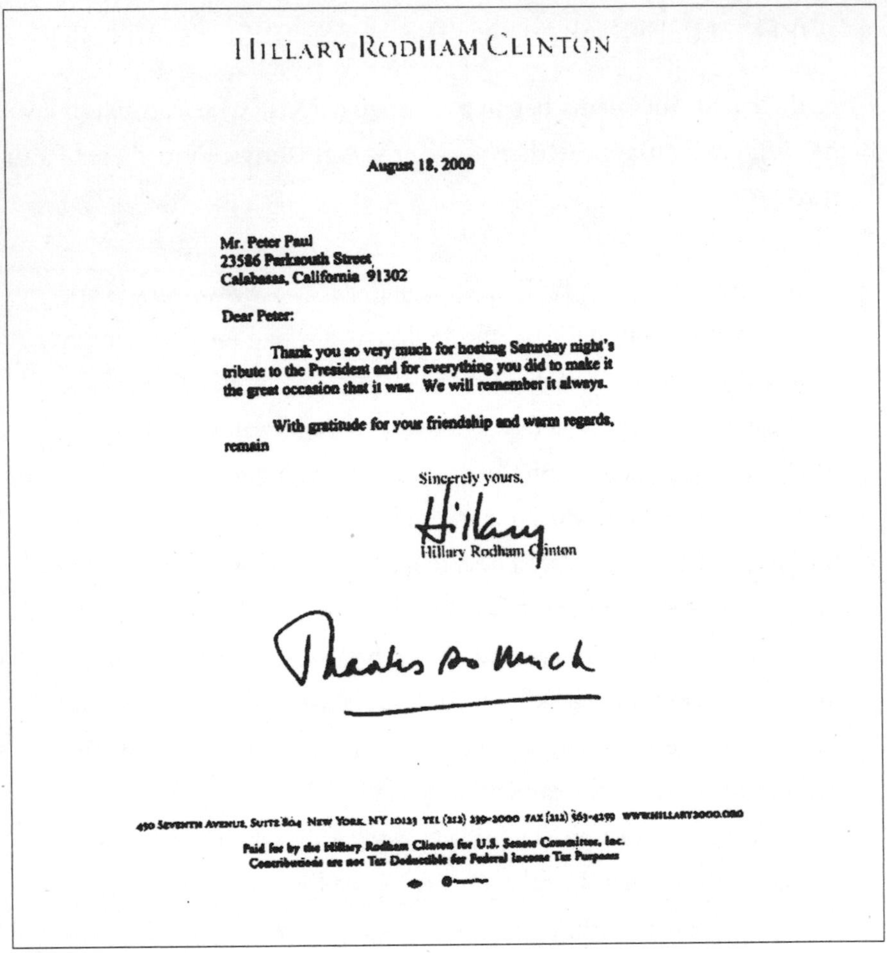

HILLARY RODHAM CLINTON

August 18, 2000

Mr. Peter Paul
23586 Parkzouth Street
Calabasas, California 91302

Dear Peter:

Thank you so very much for hosting Saturday night's tribute to the President and for everything you did to make it the great occasion that it was. We will remember it always.

With gratitude for your friendship and warm regards, remain

Sincerely yours,

Hillary

Hillary Rodham Clinton

Thanks so much

450 SEVENTH AVENUE, SUITE 804 NEW YORK, NY 10123 TEL (212) 239-2000 FAX (212) 563-4299 WWW.HILLARY2000.ORG

Paid for by the Hillary Rodham Clinton for U.S. Senate Committee, Inc.
Contributions are not Tax Deductible for Federal Income Tax Purposes

Figure 1

before the Clintons left office. They said okay. It all went fine. They allowed Mr. Oto to sit at a table adjacent to the president. There were 2,500 people there, and most didn't have good seats. But Mr. Oto was seated right next to the president's table. And afterward they gave him a private tour of the Oval Office and allowed him to sit in the president's chair and have his photo taken.

I was quite impressed by this, because I had known a lot of people who had been in the Oval Office and I'd never seen anybody get photos in the president's chair. This was a good indication that my business proposition was still on track—even though Hillary was saying publicly that she would have nothing to do with me.

But still I was nervous, given all that I was reading.

So with the help of Hillary's office, I was one of the first people to greet Bill Clinton when he arrived in Los Angeles on Air Force One five days later. Right away, we stepped to the side and he cut a video again thanking me for what I had done and telling me [he] was looking forward to working together. He also cut a video message for my wife, who was about to give birth. And I recall him saying, because it was so odd, "If we take any more pictures together, they're going to wonder who the father is." It was a very odd comment coming from the commander in chief.

So to revisit the timeline: The *Washington Post* articles came out on August 15 and 17, and in those articles the Clintons emphatically stated that they would not take any more money from me and they made a big deal of returning the $2,000 contribution. Then on August 24, I received a fax from David Rosen on Hillary Clinton for Senate letterhead asking me to transfer $100,000 in stock to a group called the "Working Family Party" (see Figure 2).

Peter Paul says, "Hillary had no problems with me as long as I was writing checks."

Set aside the bald-faced duplicity of their actions, this constituted another illegal act. Federal campaigns cannot direct contributions intended for that campaign to a non-reporting state committee— which is what the Working Family Party was. Here you have a smoking gun document, on her letterhead faxed to my controller, with the wiring instructions to send $100,000 to this group.

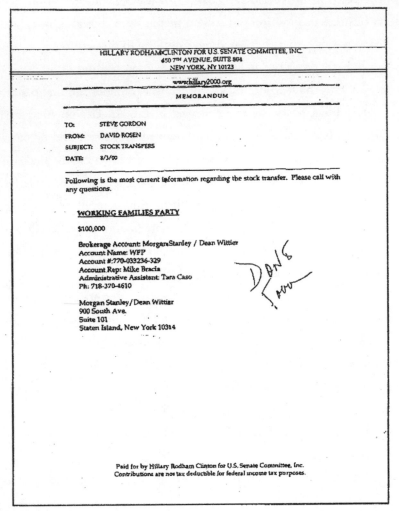

Figure 2

When the government began investigating the charges of criminal activity in the Hillary for Senate campaign, Hillary was able to obstruct their investigation and turn her finance director, David Rosen, into the fall guy. Paul explains how the trial unfolded:

If Hillary had cooperated with the investigations against her, she would have been indicted and not David Rosen. But Hillary claimed that David Rosen was the only person who knew about the cost of the event, that he withheld this information from Hillary's campaign, that as a result the campaign filed three false FEC reports.

In his trial, David Rosen's defense strategy was to paint me as a con man who withheld information on the gala costs from him.

Before the case began, the judge, who had been appointed by Bill Clinton in 1998, made a statement to the jury. He said Hillary Clinton had no role whatsoever in this matter and that the jury was not to consider Hillary at all. The judge also said that I was a totally corrupt con man. So basically the judge said to the jury that Rosen's defense was all true. That because I was a con man, David Rosen never got accurate information from me, so he couldn't be guilty of withhold-ing the information that the campaign used to file a false report.

The judge threw the case before it began.

But here's what did not come out in court: on July 17, the first day that I began actively writing checks to produce the gala, I got a phone call from Hillary Clinton. I immediately turned the video camera on to capture the moment.

That tape was taken from me in 2001 by the Eastern District U.S. Attorney in New York. I wasn't able to get it released until April of 2007. A lot of time had passed, and I had forgotten the details. When I reviewed the tape, I found Hillary's confirmation that (a) she had been fully briefed on my progress on the gala, (b) she had desig-nated her White House staff assistant to liaison with me, and (c) she would be involved on a personal basis whenever needed.

Hillary Clinton has managed to use the power she has amassed since leaving the White House to compromise all three branches of government. It's a cautionary tale for us all. Her ability to thwart inves-tigations by the Senate, Federal Election Commission, and Department of Justice, combined with her ability to induce a federal judge to throw a criminal trial by making false statements to a jury and to cause a prosecutor to exonerate her with the full knowledge that evidence existed, tells us how scary the power she has amassed has become.

The message I'm trying to communicate based on my personal experience with Hillary Clinton is that she poses a real threat to the freedoms and liberties that we as American citizens have. She's not accountable. She'll never be accountable personally for anything that she does. She believes that the ends justify the means—no matter the means.

PETER PAUL TAKES A LIE DETECTOR TEST

At this point, Peter Paul took a lie detector test, administered in accordance with North Carolina law, by polygraph expert Ray Ezell:

MR. EZELL: My purpose is to give you as good a polygraph exam as I can. I'm not here to trick you or surprise you. I will explain the procedure to you and then ask you a series of questions. You will need to stay focused. A polygraph machine is little more than a laptop computer hooked up to a printer, which will be running. You will hear it run. There are also sensory tubes—one goes around your waist; one goes around your chest. These tubes record your chest cavity movement in relation to your breathing. There are two stainless steel plates which are attached to two of your fingers. They record your galvanic skin response, your sweat gland activity. There is a cardio cuff which goes on your arm to record your pulse rate and blood volume. From these components, we pick up your body's physiology and trace it on graph paper.

The polygraph's power in obtaining truthfulness relates to your body's autonomic nervous system. This is commonly known as the "fight or flight" system—that is, when your brain perceives a dangerous situation, it activates the autonomic nervous system. That, in turn, changes your body physiology and prepares you to respond in one of three ways: fight the danger, run from it, or freeze up. Once that autonomic system is activated, the body physiology changes.

The same thing occurs when a person is not being truthful. When a person knows the truth but decides not to tell the truth, as soon as they make that decision the autonomic nervous system activates and it changes the body physiology. In most cases a person never realizes their physiology has changed. But the polygraph can see it. So be 100 percent honest in your answers. Your body doesn't know the difference between a little lie and a big lie. It just knows you're not being truthful and it reacts. Do you understand everything I've explained to you?

MR. PAUL: Yes.

MR. EZELL: Okay, all of the questions allow for simple yes and no answers. Some questions concern Hillary Clinton and President Clinton. Some questions are "known truth" questions that both you and I know the answer to, such as, "Are the lights on in this room?" I want you to listen to exactly what I'm asking you. Don't try to read anything into the question. No one question on the test is more important than any other. Wait until I've completely asked the question before you answer. My first question: Do you plan to lie to any of the questions on this test?

MR. PAUL: No.

MR. EZELL: On June 9, 2000, did you discuss with Hillary Clinton supporting her campaign in exchange for President Clinton helping you in your business concern?

MR. PAUL: Yes.

MR. EZELL: On August 12, 2000, at Kim Roberts's home, did you propose to Hillary Clinton supporting her campaign provided President Clinton helped you with your business interests?

MR. PAUL: Yes.

MR. EZELL: On August 13, 2000, at Barbra Streisand's home, did you talk with Hillary Clinton about supporting her campaign provided President Clinton helped you with your business interests?

MR. PAUL: Yes.

MR. EZELL: Did Hillary Clinton pledge President Clinton's support for your business interests?

MR. PAUL: Yes.

MR. EZELL: Did you discuss the subjects presented in these questions with President Clinton?

MR. PAUL: Yes.

MR. EZELL: Are you being completely truthful about the details of the events you describe here today?

MR. PAUL: Yes.

MR. EZELL: All right. Now these other questions are the questions that you and I both know the answer to. Is this the year 2007?

MR. PAUL: Yes.

MR. EZELL: Is this the month of August?

MR. PAUL: Yes.

MR. EZELL: Are you now sitting down?

MR. PAUL: Yes.

MR. EZELL: Is your first name Peter?

MR. PAUL: Yes.

MR. EZELL: Is your last name Paul?

MR. PAUL: Yes.

MR. EZELL: Are you now in the state of North Carolina?

MR. PAUL: Yes.

MR. EZELL: Did you answer truthfully each question on this test?

MR. PAUL: Yes.

The polygraph expert asked the same questions several times to meet the requirements for establishing truthfulness. We've omitted the repeated questions. While the polygrapher began analyzing the results, we asked Peter Paul why we should believe his version of events:

No one has ever challenged my veracity when I've given statements in any courtroom or in the media. I have numerous glowing reports of my truthfulness in testifying in various court actions. There are various assistant U.S. attorneys who have written about my veracity. I have never been charged with perjury or making a false statement in connection with any court proceeding.

Conversely, I believe it was William Safire who wrote in the *New York Times* that Hillary is a congenital liar. She can't help herself. And it was David Geffen, a very credible Hollywood producer and former supporter of hers, who commented on the ease with which she lies. When you consider this . . . it suggests a high level of credibility in the allegations I have made against her.

But don't just believe Mr. Safire and Mr. Geffen. It was the liberal *New York Observer* newspaper that editorialized that Mrs. Clinton was so corrupt as to be "unfit for elective office."

At the time Mr. Paul blew the whistle on Hillary Clinton's campaign frauds, an investigation was launched into the demise of his public company. Whether it was coincidence or not has not been established. Mr. Paul was indicted on one count of violating Securities and Exchange Rule 10b5 involving the misuse of trading accounts with Merrill Lynch. He pled guilty and was, at the time of this interview, awaiting sentencing. Given all he's been through, it is remarkable how Peter Paul continues to pursue these charges against Hillary. According to Paul:

> My family isn't happy that I've pursued this because everybody wants to get some peace and stability back in their lives. But this all began as part of what I thought was a noble deed—which was building a global company that could export motivational and inspirational stories and characters to young people around the world. And when it was perverted by these people who have gotten away with every kind of illegality, I thought I should try to hold them accountable since no one else seems to be able to.
>
> I've petitioned every agency that you can petition. I have a landmark civil fraud suit pending in California. I'm hoping through that lawsuit to expose the misconduct that ought to disqualify anybody from holding the highest office in the land.
>
> I'm not asking anybody to like me, or to trust me, or even to believe me. I'm asking people to look at the record that is undisputed and to come to their own conclusions regarding the suitability of Hillary Clinton to acquire the highest office in this country.
>
> I can't think of any politician in history who has shown such contempt for the Constitution and the rule of law as Hillary Clinton.

At this point, the polygrapher, Ray Ezell, shared his findings:

By way of background, I was a postal inspector for twenty-five years, investigating federal statutes as they pertained to the post office. In conjunction with that, I began doing polygraphs after attending the Department of Defense Polygraph Institute. That school certifies and trains all federal law enforcement examiners. I retired from the inspection service in May 1998, and in 1999 I began my own business. Since then I have administered between 1,500 to 2,000 polygraphs.

After reviewing the polygraph charts, I would conclude that Mr. Paul has been truthful in answering the questions.

THE CLINTONS' LONG HISTORY OF CAMPAIGN VIOLATIONS CONTINUES

While neither Peter Paul nor Aaron Tonken would qualify as Boy Scouts, each of them in separate interviews offered glimpses into the private world of Hillary Clinton and her willingness to break any law or any person standing between her and the presidency.

To get a different and unassailable view on Hillary's history of campaign transgressions, we turned to the recent editorial page director of the *Washington Times,* Tony Blankley:

Every few months there's another political fund-raising scandal. Hillary has been the subject of it recently. My personal belief is that it's sort of inevitable—money goes to politics. It always has. Rich people have been bribing kings since the beginning of time to get titles, to get power, and it continues today. We regulate it as best we can, but it doesn't stop the flow of money to power. So I don't get too exercised by these problems. Raising money is a necessary and difficult business in politics, just as in business.

That said, one thing to keep an eye on is when the financial irregularities keep coming from the same source. The Clintons have had a lot of trouble with Chinese money over the years. When you look at the policies of President Clinton toward China, you have to wonder if we were seeing the opening markets or secret corruption.

The Clinton-China connection has been the most enduring, stretching back from the beginning of Bill Clinton's administration to Hillary's current fund-raising with Norman Hsu, the convicted felon most recently accused of bilking investors out of millions in an elaborate Ponzi scheme and then turning that stolen cash over to Hillary's campaign. At the time of this writing, the outcome of these improprieties is still a huge unknown hanging over Hillary's campaign.

Few people know more about these kinds of Clinton campaign abuses than the man who chaired the committee investigating the Clintons in the 1990s, Congressman Dan Burton:

> The Clintons used every square foot of the White House as a fundraising device. Johnny Chung told us about a Hong Kong meeting with a woman from the Communist Chinese government. A man came in—he was the head of the Chinese equivalent of our CIA— and he told the group, "We like your president; we're going to give you $300,000 for his campaign because we want to see him reelected." Chung testified under oath about this obviously illegal campaign contribution, yet nothing ever came of it.

In her book *The Vast Right Wing Conspiracy's Dossier on Hillary Clinton*, *Townhall.com* reporter and author Amanda Carpenter has tallied up the legions of Clinton people who ran afoul of the law, beginning with Hillary herself:

The most interesting record Hillary Clinton set as First Lady was the most number of times anyone said "I do not know" in testimony before Congress. She said "I do not know" a whopping 250 times in questions dealing with controversies about her personal finances and her husband's transgressions.

Also interesting is the number of Clinton associates who pleaded guilty, or were indicted, or who fled the country with the police chasing them. There were 47 individuals and businesses affiliated with the Clintons who pleaded guilty or were convicted of crimes. There were 61 indictments and misdemeanor charges. There were 122 Congressional witnesses who took the Fifth. These numbers are unprecedented—I wouldn't be surprised if they totaled more than all previous administrations put together.

And we were given a reporter's eye view of dealing with the Clintons' financial dealings from *New York Times* reporter and Pulitzer Prize winner, Jeff Gerth:

Personally, I have the skin of a rhinoceros, so I'm not easily intimidated. I've spent thirty years doing investigative reporting for the *New York Times*, and I've written about most everything, Republicans, Democrats, this, that, and the other. But she and her husband have been pretty relentless and ferocious in how they attack. . . .

I started reporting on the Clintons in 1992. I was assigned, as part of the presidential campaign coverage, to look at their finances—both political and personal. So I went to Arkansas and did a couple of stories, the third of which was the Whitewater story. In terms of cooperation, it was negligible. Routine requests to get tax returns, which presidential candidates usually provide, were ignored. As we reported in our book, a campaign aide was told by Hillary that if she released the tax returns, she'd never work in Democratic politics again. The reason for this? Those tax returns showed her commodity trades!

She clearly has exhibited a pattern of secrecy in her Senate operations. She does not even adhere to Senate rules on disclosure of information. So if she wins, we can expect her administration to be inaccessible for most reporters, and in some ways intimidating.

HILLARY'S VICIOUS DESTRUCTION OF A MAN OF HONOR

Early in the first Clinton administration, stories surfaced of problems in the White House Travel Office. To most people it sounded like so much bureaucratic hooey. The Clintons made sure it sounded that way. But now the victim of "Travelgate," a man named Billy Dale, has come forward to tell us what really happened when the Clintons first came into office, and what we could expect if they came back into office again.

Billy Dale grew up a coal miner's son in the mountains of Virginia. One summer during high school he joined his father working in the mines, but his father told him, "If you don't finish school and leave here, your future is in a coalmine, a sawmill, or a filling station." The next time the air force recruiter came to town, Billy Dale signed up. He served four years and then bounced around a little before ending up in the White House Travel Office.

Politically, he was registered Independent because he didn't want either Democrats or Republicans to ever accuse him of favoring one over the other. He has voted both sides. As a matter of fact, he voted for Bill Clinton . . . the first time.

HURRICANE HILLARY RIPS THROUGH THE WHITE HOUSE

We caught up with Billy Dale at his retirement home on a lake in southern Virginia:

I first began working as a career staffer at the White House in 1961 with John Kennedy. Bill Clinton was the eighth president I worked for. I was by then director of the White House Travel Office, responsible for providing travel services for the employees of the White House, agencies that reported to the White House, and the White House Press Corps when the president traveled. We provided schedules, ticketing, reservations, you name it.

There were only seven of us in the office, so we often worked long days. It wasn't uncommon when we were traveling to work eighteen-hour days. It was a very trying job, a lot of headaches. But to stay there for thirty-two years—you could say I enjoyed it!

I had strong feelings for my country. I can remember one time we went to Moscow with the president. We'd arrived about an hour before Air Force One was due; we were waiting for the president and looking around at the terminal in the background. Flying up alongside the Russian flag was the American flag. Air Force One came in, and they played the "Star Spangled Banner," and chills ran up my spine. It was such a tremendous feeling being there as an American and knowing the freedom that we have in this country—or thought we had—until we were betrayed by the Clintons.

When each new administration comes in, they are free to fire any of the career staff they choose, but that usually doesn't happen. Career staffs provide needed continuity between administrations. And generally, the political types who come in with a new administration don't want the type of jobs we have—there's not much glory in them.

When Bill Clinton was elected, we knew we were in for a rougher transition than usual. We had heard stories from Secret Service agents and rumors that the Clintons wanted to bring in a travel agency from Little Rock. Our first real clue what lay ahead came on inauguration day. I received a phone call from a lady asking for Catherine Cornelius. I told her there was nobody in our office by that name. The caller was quite surprised. She'd been told that Catherine was taking over.

Turns out, Ms. Cornelius first went to work in the administrative offices of David Watkins, answering phones. She was twenty-four years old, apparently a cousin of President Clinton. In the last week of March, David Watkins called [me] and asked if I would give Ms. Cornelius a job and teach her the ropes so she could become a travel agent some day. Well, the handwriting was now on the wall. But I said we'd be happy to help.

It happened that I was having stomach problems at that time. My doctor said it was job-related stress and told me to take a week off. The week coincided with Ms. Cornelius reporting to work in our office. I had briefed all the guys and told them to make her feel welcome.

When I came back to work the following Monday, my assistant pulled me aside and showed me a copy of a check I had written to PanAm Airlines for a press charter. The check was for $250,000, and it was three or four years old. My assistant told me that when he had come to work the previous Friday morning, the copy machine was badly jammed and couldn't be cleared. So he had called in a tech, and it was the tech who found the check. My assistant asked, "Has this been here all that time?" The tech said, "No, this is what jammed the machine."

So when Ms. Cornelius came in that day, my assistant showed the check to her and asked if she knew anything about it. She denied knowing anything. Only later did we learn from FBI investigators that she was coming back to the office after it closed at night, rifling through our records, copying things, and taking some records home with her.

There was nothing we could do, though, since she openly boasted that she could get the president on the phone anytime she wanted. So we gave her a desk and basically ignored her. It wasn't hard, because she wasn't in much, and when she was, she spent most the time e-mailing her boyfriend. When she would take a call from a staff member wanting a travel reservation, she would walk the information over to the desk of someone else to do the work.

In the meantime, I received the most unusual phone call from a fellow in Ohio. He said he was with a travel charter company, and he wanted to know how he could "get in on some of the White House charter business." I told him that the charter business was my job—the White House paid me to do it.

I know now that he was partners with Harry Thomasson, a friend of Bill and Hillary's from Hollywood. But I didn't know who Harry Thomasson was at that time, and didn't know this fellow.

I tried to be courteous, I listened to him at length, and finally when I couldn't get rid of him, I told him, "Look, I've got work to do. What's in this for you?" He replied that "naturally we're going to make a commission when you call me to arrange a charter for the president." I'm trying to be civil with the guy. I said, "That's what this office does. We arrange the charters. Calling you would be a duplication of efforts!" And he said, "I know, but we could make some money here!" At that point, I ended the call.

After he hung up, I suppose he called his pal Harry Thomasson, and then Harry Thomasson called his pals Hillary and Bill and told them he had uncovered wrongdoing in the travel office.

CLINTON'S FRIENDS WANTED TO BILK THE TAXPAYERS

As Mr. Dale's story unfolded, we became transfixed at the differences between what he was telling us and what the Washington papers had reported at the time. He continued:

> I don't know if things might have turned out differently if I had been dishonest and made "an arrangement" with this fellow from Ohio. But I did know our time was limited, and I was getting close to retirement age anyway, so I figured why not [retire]? I went to David Watkins and gave notice, effective June 1. Oddly, he asked me to hold off on the announcement for a few days because "we have some plans for the travel office, and they will be completed in the next few days."
>
> So I went back and briefed everybody. Some of the guys started getting their resumés together. Then that Friday, Patsy Thomasson walked in and said she was there to audit the travel office. The auditors were young people from the Peat Marwick accounting firm. They were there all day asking questions, requesting records. Some I could provide; some I could not—because records were missing. We assumed that they were missing because Ms. Cornelius had taken them home, but we had no proof.

After the FBI became involved in this investigation, Ms. Cornelius did in fact turn over the records in question. But at the time, Billy Dale was stuck between a rock and kin of the president:

> I prided myself on keeping organized files. At any time if you had asked me to get a file for a certain trip, I was able to retrieve it within ten minutes. I had a system; I would keep all the year's petty cash logs in a loose-leaf binder. At year's end, I would put them all in a big

manila envelope for storage. But in the audit, we found one manila envelope missing. Because it was missing, I couldn't account for $14,000 in checks that had been written for cash the previous year.

Soon thereafter David Watkins called a 10:30 a.m. meeting. He told us that we were going to be let go because Clinton had promised to reduce the White House staff by 25 percent. We were part of the 25 percent, and they wanted us out of the building by noon.

At the same time David Watkins was telling us we were being let go because of Clinton's promise, DeeDee Myers was telling the Press Corps that we were being fired for criminal misconduct and that the FBI had been called in to conduct a criminal investigation.

I was accused of embezzling the $14,000.

Whether we were fired to eliminate waste in government, or on charges of embezzlement—either way, we were blindsided.

White House employees flooded our office, wondering what was going on. It was all over the news. Our home phone was ringing off the hook. We filled up two cassette tapes in the answering machine of people wanting us to call back. One of our neighbors came in to answer the phone for us. It was a terrible day.

ALL THEY HAD TO DO WAS FIRE BILLY

It's hard to understand how Travelgate escalated so fast. All the Clintons had to do was say, "Billy, we're going to let you and your staff go." But the Clintons had several plans brewing at the same time, as Billy Dale explains:

There had been a lot of negative news reporting on the Clintons. They thought that if they could concoct some story showing how they were cleaning up waste, fraud, and abuse at the White House, it would look good for them. And that's what they did.

The morning after we were blindsided, and I was out of work with no idea what I faced, I received a call from Larry Speaks, former press secretary to President Reagan and an old friend. He said, "Billy, have you got an attorney?" And I said, "Why do I need an attorney? I haven't done anything wrong." And Larry says, "Bill, I suggest you get an attorney. I know Fred Fielding, who used to be Reagan's counsel." So I said, "Go ahead and call him."

Fielding's office was nearby the White House. I walked in, told him what had happened, and he advised, "Don't talk to anybody. I'll put the word out that I'm your attorney, and all inquiries should come to me."

I was indicted on December 9, 1994, though I knew the day before that the indictment was coming down. So I got up early that morning to drive to the 7-Eleven to get a newspaper. I got up before dawn, hadn't even combed my hair, just put a baseball cap on and walked out the door. Klieg lights lit up all around. There was a van from CBS News parked out front. They jumped out. So I just walked around to the back of the house and ignored them.

One of the cameramen in the van sent word to me afterward. He told me how he had tried to get off the assignment. He had told his boss, "I know Billy Dale. I have traveled around the world with this man, and I would prefer you send somebody else." And they told him, "You go or your job goes." I got phone calls from people like that all the time.

My most immediate problem was money. I had $40,000 at most in a savings account. I told Fred Fielding that I wouldn't be able to afford his legal fees. And he said, "You shouldn't worry—this is family." So when I left the White House I had approximately forty-five days of annual leave accumulated, which they paid me for. I got a check in June for $8,300. I later got a bill from Fred Fielding for $8,100 and heard that he wrote off $180,000 in legal bills.

I had no idea how I was going to get through this financially. I remember going to the grocery store with my wife, Blanche. I was following along behind her and she would put a can of brand-name vegetables in the cart and I would replace it with a generic brand, which was four or five cents cheaper, because I was looking for every way to save money, not knowing what I still had to face.

In addition to the indictment, there was an IRS audit that wouldn't have happened unless someone high in government wanted it to happen. The FBI just showed up at my daughter's office and served a subpoena. My daughter-in-law pulled into her driveway after work one night and a car pulled in behind her—it was an FBI agent serving a subpoena. There was nothing I could do. I would just sit in my front yard and watch the traffic go by, hoping the telephone wouldn't ring, but not feeling at liberty to stray far from it. I would get phone calls from friends who wanted to meet somewhere to talk—they were afraid to talk over a line that could be tapped. This hell went on for thirty months. . . .

Attorneys told me the cost of going to trial and defending myself would be about a half-million dollars, in addition to the legal bills I had already run up. I had to make a decision whether I wanted to go to court and spend that kind of money, money I did not have.

Blanche and I had been married for thirty-eight years; could I ask her to give up everything we had worked for?

I figured it would be easier to come up with $69,000, go to jail for three to six months, and get this hell behind me. So I decided to tell the judge that I was guilty, and then go to the courthouse steps and tell the press that I had pleaded guilty to something that I was not guilty of and the reason that I had done it. And my attorney told me, "You cannot do that. The very minute you come out and say you lied, the judge will jerk you back into court and charge you with perjury, and you'll spend even more time in jail."

I suppose I was naïve to the law, but not to principle. So I said, "Let's go to court."

My memories of the trial are vague. I was in a constant fog and couldn't concentrate on a thing. Had it had not been for our church and our minister who surrounded the whole family, I don't know how we would have gotten through.

We were all very nervous. My oldest daughter was pregnant with her first child. I remember her telling me, when we thought I was going to jail, that she would sit staring at the calendar, trying to decide what days she would be able to take off after the baby was born so she could bring him to the prison, wherever I was, to visit with me.

I remember my oldest daughter telling Blanche that if I was found guilty and had to go to jail, she didn't know if she could live in this country any longer. How could people in our government do something like this? She didn't know.

It was very hard on Blanche. When we moved from Maryland to a new home, I had some White House pictures that had been on the wall, and I was putting them on the wall of our new home. She told me no, you can't put those up. She didn't want anything that remotely reminded her of the White House. This after a thirty-two-year career that we had all been proud of.

Shortly after I was fired, my father, who was eighty-nine years old, veered his car across the center divider into a truck carrying thirty-five tons of coal. The truck broadsided him, pushed him into a metal guard railing. They had to cut him out of the car. He was crushed from his chest down and never recovered. I often wonder why he pulled across the road in front of that truck. Was he not paying attention? Was he worried about me? I've never been able to answer that.

All during the long trial, I had to call the court once a week to let them know I was still in town. I was not free to travel more than one hundred miles without the court's permission. Well, my brother who lived in Georgia developed leukemia, and the hospital asked if I could come in to give a blood sample to see if I was compatible for a bone marrow transplant. I had to get my attorney to call the courthouse, and it took two days to get approval. It was infuriating to be told I wasn't free to help my brother.

The long and the short of the trial: the Justice Department could not after a thirty-month investigation find anybody to testify against me. Six people from the travel office were on the witness list. After calling two of them, the prosecutor decided that their testimony was more beneficial to the defense than to him, so he didn't call the others. We had members of the White House Press Corps coming in as character witnesses. People from every one of the networks and the major newspapers came in. Finally, the judge said he didn't need to hear any more.

On the last day of the trial, the judge gave instructions to the jury and then released us, saying we would be notified when they had a verdict. We had just arrived back at the attorney's office when we got a telephone call to report back to courthouse. The jury had deliberated less than an hour. They found me not guilty on all counts.

And I laid my head down on the desk and cried.

Even after the trial was completed, the Clintons continued their stealthy attacks on Billy Dale:

Once the trial was over, the IRS came to audit my income tax returns. This gentleman showed up at my house one morning. He introduced himself, and he said, "Mr. Dale, before I come in, I want to apologize to you for being here. I've been ordered to go over your income tax records, and I would rather be anyplace else in the world right now. But I've got fourteen months until I can retire, and I have to follow orders."

We spent the whole day going over my financial records, my bank accounts, and when he left he said, "Mr. Dale, I don't think you have anything to worry about." A couple of weeks later, I received a letter from him telling me that my taxes were in order.

HILLARY'S CENTRAL ROLE IN THE DESPICABLE ACT

In the course of the trial and events thereafter, a lot was learned about who was most responsible for the thirty months of hell unleashed willy-nilly on Billy Dale:

We learned that Hillary was much more involved than Bill. Her notes showed that she asked about the matter regularly at staff meetings; she gave direction to her subordinates; she coordinated the legal strategy.

When it blew up in her face, Hillary went on the TV news shows trying to justify the firings. She was questioned a lot. She always claimed that there was mismanagement and wrongdoing. Once on the *Larry King Show* I looked into the camera and asked her to tell me what I did wrong. She never replied, of course. But I would still like her to tell me what I did to justify her full-court attack on me and my family.

Nobody who worked with our travel office reported any mismanagement and wrongdoing.

An FBI investigation found no evidence of mismanagement and wrongdoing.

An IRS audit found no mismanagement and wrongdoing.

A jury found no mismanagement and wrongdoing—*at least not on Billy Dale's part.*

But the independent counsel who looked into the whole matter determined that Hillary's testimony was less than forthright. His official report noted this:

> "It is, in the Independent Counsel's judgment, beyond peradventure that as a matter of historical fact, Mrs. Clinton's input into the process was a significant—if not the significant—factor influencing the pace of events in the Travel Office firings and the ultimate decision to fire the employees. Accordingly, the Independent Counsel concludes that Mrs. Clinton's sworn testimony that she had no input into Watkins's decision or role in the Travel Office firings is factually incorrect" (Independent Counsel's final report re: The White House Travel Office).

Author Ann Coulter discusses the independent counsel's finding that Mrs. Clinton gave false statements under oath:

> I mean, really, it's shocking that—that any elected official, much less the president of the United States [and] his lovely wife, now a senator, would so hold the legal system in such contempt.
>
> I mean, Americans really need to understand, without the rule of law, it is the rule of the jungle; it is the powerful over the weak. The rule of law is what protects us in this country. That's why, a large part of the reason why, it is meaningful to be an American, and go any place in the world and say, "I am an American." Because we believe in the rule of law, that we are governed only by our consent, and not that someone has some divine right to rule over us, as apparently Hillary thinks she does.

In speaking to people who observed Hillary during the Travelgate period, there is a sadness that at first surfaces, a sadness that turns to contempt as they recall how viciously Hillary ripped into Billy Dale.

Former *Washington Times* editorial director Tony Blankley considers Travelgate the defining face of the Clinton years:

> There are many events in the Clintons' political history worth recalling before you vote for Hillary. A small example, but a telling one, involved the White House Travel Office. You had career civil servants doing a great job as travel agents for the president and his staff. But the Clintons wanted to get a lackey friend in. They could have fired the guy in charge. No problem. But instead, they accused him of a crime. They tried to ruin his life in order to get their lackeys in.
>
> The head of the Travel Office was tried and acquitted within a matter of hours by the jury. That's the cynicism and ruthlessness of the Clintons. And a lot of people thought Hillary took the lead in trumping up the charges.

Blankley's sentiments are echoed by Congressman Dan Burton:

> It was an all-time low! Billy Dale and the people in the Travel Office were castigated and accused of illegal activity by Hillary Clinton— and there was no basis for it. Hillary went after them because she wanted to put her friends in charge of the Travel Office. When the case came to trial, they were found totally innocent of any wrongdoing. The case was practically dismissed out of hand because there was no evidence. Billy Dale and his people were finally vindicated, but not before the Clintons had ruined their lives.

Dealing with people as ruthless and ambitious as the Clintons was quite a deal for a coal miner's son, Billy Dale:

> When the Clintons were still in office, I didn't feel comfortable telling the whole story for fear of further retribution. I guarded my

words very carefully. But I thought that once the eight years were over and they were out of the office, I could relax a little bit. Now I know I can't.

She's an evil person.

I don't hate her; I simply despise her.

Here's another example of the real Hillary. One day after I was fired, I was walking down 17th Street on the way to my lawyer's. I passed the New Executive Office Building and saw a White House policeman on duty at the parking garage there. I had remembered him from the White House, and we got to talking. After a bit, he told me what had happened to him.

He had been posted at the elevator in the East Wing that goes up to the living quarters. At that post, there's a log of everyone who goes up on that elevator. Dates and times are kept meticulously—always have been—for security reasons. One day Hillary had some people with her, and she told him not to log them. He said okay but then dutifully logged them later on—knowing he could get in trouble if he didn't. The next day or so, Hillary found out. She went to the powers that be, raised Cain, and the White House police had him reassigned. She also told them, "If I ever see him in the East Wing again, I'll have his job." So because of Hillary, he was working the parking garage.

I've heard many stories like that from people stuck in service positions under Hillary. So when I think about four or eight more years of the Clintons, and who they might destroy this time around for their own selfish gains, I am deeply saddened.

———————————————— | 3 | ————————————————

PHYSICALLY ATTACKED
BY THE PRESIDENT

Even the most steadfast supporters of the Clintons blush and shake their heads at the sleaze Bill Clinton foisted upon us. And who hasn't wondered why Hillary Clinton put up with it? Many people believe she stayed with him in hopes he could help her get elected someday. What's less well-known is the active role Hillary played in enabling her husband's sexual appetite. One person who knows too well is Kathleen Willey of southern Virginia. She had been one of the Clintons' most loyal supporters:

> I first met Bill Clinton in 1989 at a political fund-raiser in Trussville, Alabama. My father-in-law was a senator for many years, and my husband would always run the campaign. So I just joined in. I really liked politics. My first impression of Bill Clinton was a good one—he was friendly, outgoing, nice, knowledgeable. He definitely had that charisma that everybody talks about.
>
> My first personal interaction was a couple years later at a debate at the University of Richmond. I was part of the delegation that greeted him at the airport. There were a number of us standing behind a rope

line. He came over and started talking to us, real friendly, and I noticed that he was looking at me more than other people.

Well, anyway, he got into the limo, and no sooner were they pulling away when this beautiful woman, Nancy Hernwright, came over and said, "The governor would like you and your husband's phone number." I was really pleased because none of the volunteers could get tickets to the presidential debate, and I thought this might be a chance. I even called my husband and told him we might get tickets.

No sooner did I walk in the door to my house, when the phone rang. It was Bill Clinton! I thought, *That was fast.*

Now, he had been talking so much he had laryngitis. I was concerned because he needed his voice for the big debate the next day. He said he'd be okay; he was going to see a doctor.

I said, "It sounds like you could use some chicken soup," and he replied, "That's sounds like a good idea. Could you bring me some?" And I paused and then said sure, I could drop some off. So he said, "I have to find out where Hillary is going to be tonight, and I am surrounded by Secret Service; let me just check into a few things and call you back."

Now I was thinking, *All right, you're a smart woman, you know what this is about.* So I called my husband and repeated the conversation to him. He said, "Well, what does that mean?" and I replied, "You're a man, you tell me." Neither of us was sure what to do. There had been some speculation about Clinton's womanizing, but I was a loyal Democrat and would not allow myself to even consider that it was true or relevant.

So I just waited for Clinton's call, hoping to at least finagle some debate tickets.

Sure enough, Clinton called right back and let me know that he had cleared the decks, he found out where Hillary was going to be, and to bring over that chicken soup.

At this point, I said, "I don't think I'd better do that." And that was the end of the chicken soup episode.

Turns out, I saw him the very next day at a big rally in Richmond. I had gone with my mother and a friend. We just bulldozed our way up to the rope line; my mom and my friend wanted to meet the man we hoped would be the next president of the United States. The Secret Service came first and told us not to engage him in conversation, just to shake his hand and nothing more.

So I shook Hillary's hand.

Then came Bill. He looked at my mother, who was getting rather giddy, then he looked at me, then back at my mother. Then he took his hand and started rubbing it through my hair, while looking at my mother and saying, "It's obvious why she's so pretty." Well, my mother nearly collapsed at that. Then he shook my hand for quite some time and gave me the look—the Clinton eye sweep.

And as he continued down the rope line, the whole time he kept looking back at me. My friend asked, "Do you see the way he is looking at you?" and I agreed it was pretty intense.

Finally he worked his way back to the limo, and at the last possible chance, he hopped up on this wall and pointed at me with a huge big good-bye wave. My friend and I later decided that maybe some of those rumors about him were true. But I just filed it away, not wanting to believe it.

ALL EXCITED ABOUT WORKING IN
THE CLINTON WHITE HOUSE

When Clinton won the presidency, the Willey family celebrated. They had supported him. They had raised money for him. And when an opportunity arose to volunteer to help in the White House, Kathleen Willey stepped up:

I thought this would be a nice opportunity because my children were going to college, and my husband had his law practice. So I made the commute by train.

The Monday after Easter they held the annual Egg Roll, and I saw him at yet another rope line. I congratulated him for winning and told him I was volunteering in the Correspondence Office.

Well, he said that wasn't a good place for me. And once again, I was no sooner in the door that night when Nancy Hernwright was calling to say the president wanted to meet with me the next day. As I got off the phone, again I thought, *Hmm, that was fast.*

Next day at the White House, the president greeted me with a big bear hug and then offered a private tour of the White House.

It was so overwhelming; I got caught up in the moment.

He was pointing out different things in the Oval Office, showing me the famous Remington, the John Kennedy desk. That was really something for me because I was raised Catholic, and in my little Catholic world, Kennedy was a huge hero. I kept thinking to myself, *Remember everything because when you walk out you're going to forget it all.*

So then he said, "Let me take you back to my private study," and off we went. As he closed the door, I didn't feel right. I just blurted out that "I had to leave," and I got out of there before anything could happen.

Little did I know that a whole lot was about to happen.

My husband asked me to meet him at home a few days later in the middle of the day—a first for my hardworking lawyer husband. Turns out, he had illegally borrowed money from clients. We had to cosign a note for a quarter-million dollars, and it had to be done that day. There were a lot of questions and screaming, and then my husband went off to deal with the mess.

That night he took his life. He left a note saying he was a fool out of control. He apologized to the children, and my whole world crashed. I was desperate. . . . So I made an appointment to see Bill Clinton, hoping he could help me get a job somewhere, anywhere. . . .

When I sat down at the desk in front of the president, I was upset. I was crying and telling him I needed a job and could he help?

He said he could see how upset I was and asked if I'd like a cup of coffee. I said yes, and he led us into his kitchen. I noticed that the steward had slipped out the back, and we were alone. So I turned around and headed back to the Oval Office. He said, "Just spend a few minutes in here in my private study." I was distraught, and I really needed his help. I was bawling. He could see how upset I was. At one point I thanked him for listening, told him I knew how busy he was, and started back toward the Oval Office.

Next thing I knew, Bill Clinton was all over me. It came out of nowhere. He was blurting how he had wanted to do this ever since he first met me. He's a big man. He's strong. His hands were everywhere on me. I mean he was forceful. I'm kind of little, but I wasn't afraid at this point. I was actually embarrassed for him. I was going to have to get out of there, somehow.

He finally had me pushed up into a corner, and at the same time his assistant was banging on the door because he was due in a cabinet meeting and everyone was gathering in the Oval Office.

But Bill Clinton didn't move away. His face was beet red—it was kind of like a rush he had. I finally broke free of him, and I stopped and turned around and said the silliest thing. I said, "Thank you for taking the time to see me, Mr. President." I remember thinking later, *Yes, thank you for your hands all over me, and pushing me back into the corner, and brutalizing me.*

And I kept thinking, *Who was going to be on the other side of that door into the Oval Office?* I was all messed up, makeup all over my face. Sure enough, I open the door, and there's Lloyd Benson and Leon Panetta and the entire Cabinet waiting for this meeting. I just got out of there.

FORCED TO TESTIFY IN THE PAULA JONES TRIAL

Time passed and Kathleen Willey was getting her life back together. But then she was called to give a deposition in the Paula Jones sexual harassment lawsuit against Bill Clinton. It was the last thing she wanted to do. But she was given no choice:

Two days before the deposition, I was walking in the neighborhood, and I was wearing one of those big neck collars because I'd just had surgery on my neck. It was January 8. From down the road came a jogger. He came right up to me and said, "Hello, Kathleen, did you ever find your cat?" I figured he must be a neighbor because I had put the word out when my cat disappeared a few months before. And I said no, I hadn't found him, and I really missed him. Then the jogger said rather ominously, "Yeah, that Bullseye was a really nice cat." I felt the hair stand up in the back of my neck. Something was going on.

I got spooked and demanded, "What do you want? Who are you?" He didn't answer; he just asked, "How are your children, Shannon and Patrick?" Now I was frightened. I had three dogs with me, but he didn't show any sign of being afraid of them. He just said, "You aren't getting the message, are you?"

I thought he was going to shoot me. My first thought was, *He has a gun in his pocket, and he's going to shoot me.* A lot of guys go hunting near my home, and nobody would think twice about hearing gunshots. I turned and ran as fast as I could, which was definitely not a good thing with that cervical collar on.

THE INTIMIDATION TACTICS DIDN'T LET UP

We asked Kathleen Willey if any other intimidation tactics had been used against her and if she knew who was responsible:

In September, my car had been vandalized—flat tires. At the service station they asked me to come back and take a look. The car was up on the lift. "Do you have any enemies?" the mechanic asked. "Somebody shot three of your tires out with a nail gun."

There hadn't been any construction in my area—no obvious reasons for this. I knew something was happening.

I was also being followed. I'd go into shops in Richmond where I had been all my life, and people would go in the store after I left and ask questions about me. I discovered somebody under my house at about three o'clock in the morning, and I let my dogs out after him. Another one of my cats was killed and left on my porch.

Even then I refused to believe what was happening to me. Refused to believe that a woman in this country could be facing this kind of intimidation. Refused to believe that the powers-that-be in Washington would be capable of this kind of horror.

All I could think to do was stay as far away from the Clintons as possible. But clearly that wasn't going to be possible—I had been called to give a deposition in the Paula Jones trial. I didn't want to do it, but I didn't have a choice. So I went to my local attorney to prepare, and he sat me down and explained that I was going to need a bigger attorney.

I asked him why, because I knew I hadn't done anything wrong.

I'll never forget the look on his face. He told me I would need an attorney who was good with people who commit perjury. I was floored. Perjury? And then it all started to become clear. I was going to be forced to testify in the Paula Jones case, about which I knew nothing. And Clinton's attorneys were going to make me perjure myself somehow.

Then the noose tightened. Bob Bennett, Clinton's personal attorney, offered to represent me. Wasn't that the height?! He told me that money would be no object; all of my legal bills would be covered. I wouldn't have to worry about a thing. I declined.

Came the day of the deposition. Federal judge's chambers on a Saturday morning, to avoid the press. Bob Bennett and his team of attorneys, my attorney, the judge, and a cameraman. My attorney took me into a jury room, sat me down, and just looked at me and said, "Are you ready for this?" and I said, "I guess I am." So in we went.

I started telling them my story in all its graphic detail. Bob Bennett was stunned, speechless. The questions he asked me were not forceful at all.

Then after a lunch break, we came back in, and right away Bob Bennett's cell phone rang. He answered it, "Yes, sir." And he said to us, "Excuse me, my client is on the phone." It's obvious that they had planned this. Bill Clinton was calling just to let us know that he was keeping an eye on things, and I heard Bob Bennett say, "Yes, sir, I will certainly give her your best."

When we finished that day, Bob Bennett did not say good-bye. All the niceness that he'd shown to me in previous meetings was gone. He stormed out because I didn't cave.

Two mornings later, I got up to let my dogs out and opened my front door—and sitting on the porch, facing the door, was a small animal skull. I just knew it was my cat. They had hit me again! There and then in my anger at these despicable people and their scare tactics, I decided I was never going to cave.

At this point, Kathleen Willey went on *60 Minutes* to tell her story:

Going on *60 Minutes* was tough, but finally I had my side of the story out, and all of the Clintons' lies were exposed. Of course, as a result the phone was ringing off the hook, so I was ignoring it. But I got an anonymous phone call from a private investigator named Jared Stern. He left a message advising me to be quiet and careful, because people were out to get me. He thought he needed to warn me.

Turns out, he had been hired to come down here and hurt me, and he felt so uncomfortable about it. I didn't even learn who he was until a long time afterward. He went on ABC News and said he was aware of the scare tactics being used against me.

I also got a call from Clinton's friend Nathan Landau. I had worked with his daughter in the White House Social Office; we were friends. He flew me up to see her at his beautiful estate in eastern Maryland. At one point he worked the conversation around to the Oval Office attack. That's when he suggested, "You don't have to tell anybody anything. Only two people really know what happened in there. We just do not need to talk about this."

He was strong-arming me, and he wasn't happy when I didn't cave.

He was very influential in the Democratic Party, and it's not hard to guess who put him up to it.

Only later did I learn that it was this same Nathan Landau who hired the private investigators to intimidate and threaten me.

When my story started coming out, a woman came up to me in the mall. She did not tell me who she was, but she said, "I just want to thank you for doing what you did. The same thing happened to me when I first started working, and I was young." And she broke down in tears. For years, she had blamed herself.

Other women have called and talked to me about their experiences with Bill Clinton. They said he did similar things to them as he did to me. I've asked them why they wouldn't go public with their stories. Not a single one of them would. They were too embarrassed. Too afraid.

CONTINUING A LONG HISTORY
OF ATTACKING "THE WOMEN"

These women had reason to be afraid. We obtained a memo written during the 1992 campaign by then Clinton private investigator Jack Palladino. The memo strategized about Gennifer Flowers, who disclosed an affair with Bill Clinton earlier in the campaign. The memo states in pertinent part: "Ms. Flowers—who may well re-emerge as an issue later in the campaign—should be treated as an adverse witness; exhaustive efforts should be made to impeach her character and veracity until she is destroyed beyond all resurrection."

And Jack Paladino was only one of many thugs the Clintons hired to silence the women ensnared by Bill Clinton.

Jared Stern, mentioned above by Kathleen Willey, is a private investigator who was hired by Bob Miller, who did "off the books" projects for Democrats, including ones with close ties to the Clintons. Stern could not answer many of the questions we asked him, because he would not jeopardize his reputation for maintaining the confidences of his clients. But he could answer enough.

CITIZENS UNITED: Do you know of any intimidation tactics that were going to be used against Kathleen Willey?

STERN: I suggested some tactical solutions, and I was assured that those were being taken care of by someone else.

CITIZENS UNITED: Did you speak to Kathleen Willey?

STERN: No. I left a message on her answering service.

CITIZENS UNITED: Do you believe Kathleen Willey's accounts of attacks by Bill Clinton?

STERN: I believe Kathleen Willey's accounts are 100 percent truthful and correct.

CITIZENS UNITED: How do you feel about the attempts to defame Kathleen Willey's character?

STERN: It makes me feel truly sympathetic and helpless.

CITIZENS UNITED: Another investigator before you, Jack Palladino, sent a memo to the Clintons asking if "the purpose of their investigation was to impeach Gennifer Flowers's character and veracity until she is destroyed beyond all recognition?" (See Figure 3.)

STERN: What happened to Kathleen Willey and to Gennifer Flowers is fully consistent with a continuous and regular set of Clinton tactical protocols in furtherance of their personal interests. No one will ever say that what happened to Kathleen Willey was an anomaly. That M.O. can be seen throughout the Clintons' political lives, and is consistent. The Clintons are a unit. They share a zeal for power and a willingness to engage in any and all threat neutralizing strategies—legality be damned. That makes them wrong for America.

CITIZENS UNITED: Have you been afraid for your career or your safety as a result of this?

STERN: I generally try to maintain a healthy level of near-debilitating paranoia, so the short answer is yes. And particularly while Clinton was president, yes.

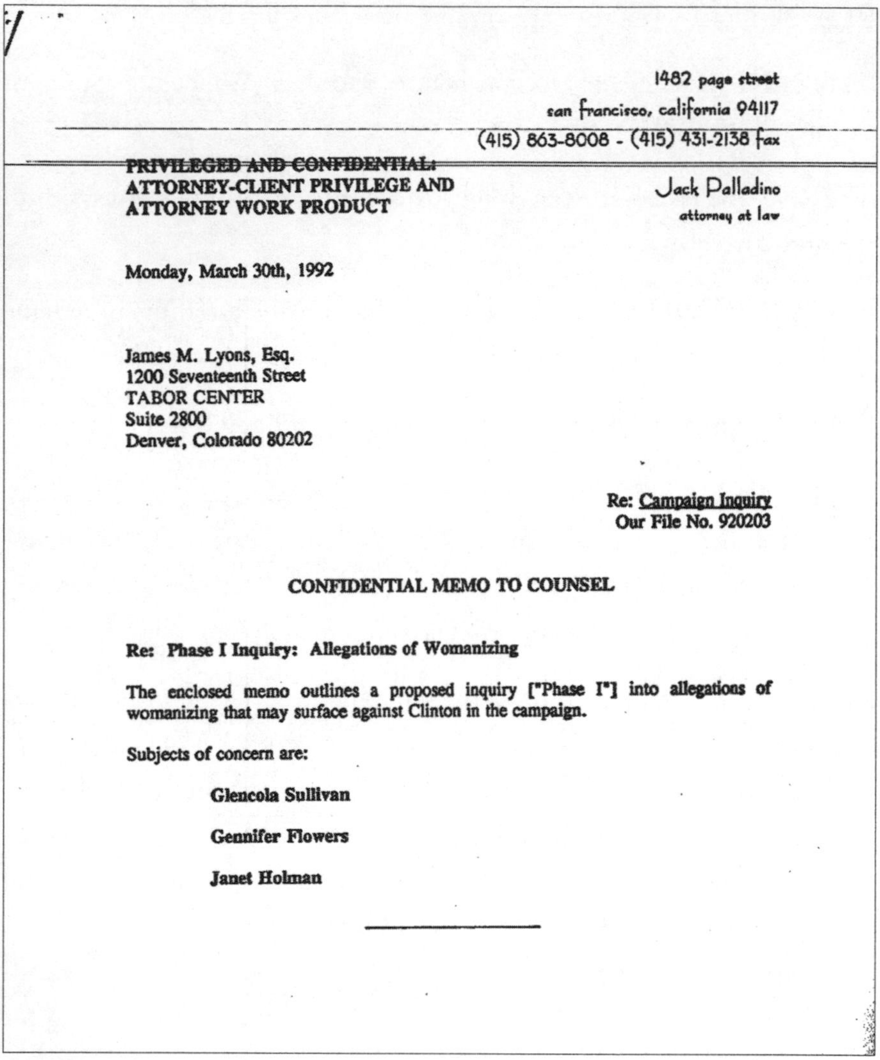

1482 page street
san francisco, california 94117
(415) 863-8008 - (415) 431-2138 fax

PRIVILEGED AND CONFIDENTIAL:
ATTORNEY-CLIENT PRIVILEGE AND
ATTORNEY WORK PRODUCT

Jack Palladino
attorney at law

Monday, March 30th, 1992

James M. Lyons, Esq.
1200 Seventeenth Street
TABOR CENTER
Suite 2800
Denver, Colorado 80202

Re: Campaign Inquiry
Our File No. 920203

CONFIDENTIAL MEMO TO COUNSEL

Re: Phase I Inquiry: Allegations of Womanizing

The enclosed memo outlines a proposed inquiry ["Phase I"] into allegations of womanizing that may surface against Clinton in the campaign.

Subjects of concern are:

Glencola Sullivan

Gennifer Flowers

Janet Holman

Figure 3

One author who has focused on the private side of the Clintons is Edward Klein. He wrote *The Truth About Hillary: What She Knew, When She Knew It, and How Far She'll Go to Become President* (Sentinel, 2005). And having dug deep, Klein has found a less flattering portrait of Hillary than we were meant to see, especially when it comes to the use of thugs:

Jack Palladino, Esq.

James M. Lyons, Esq.   March 30th, 1992
Re: Campaign Inquiry   Page 3

Re: Gennifer G. Flowers [42]
    Soc. Sec: 432-98-9178
    DOB: 1/24/50 (Oklahoma City)

    9030 Markville Drive
    #4116
    Dallas, Texas 75243
    (214) 238-9917   (circa 1984)

Ms. Flowers - who may well re-emerge as an issue later in the campaign - should be treated as an adverse witness; exhaustive efforts should be made to impeach her character and veracity until she is destroyed beyond all resurrection. As part of that effort, every acquaintance, employer, and past lover should be located and interviewed.

I do not propose we do so out of vengeance but rather because I suspect we have not heard the last from Ms. Flowers in this campaign. Furthermore, she is now a shining icon - telling lies that so far have proved all benefit and no cost - for any other opportunist who may be considering making Clinton a target. Finally, a full expose of Ms. Flowers (perhaps authored by a friendly reporter) might serve as an illustration of the hypocrisy and failure of the press.

―――――――――――

Flowers grew up in Brinkley, Arkansas. Her father, Jim Flowers, is deceased; her mother has remarried:

        Mary Hirst
        Missouri
        (417) 739-4445

―――――――――――

Figure 3, continued

I've interviewed Ivan Duda—a well-known detective in Little Rock. He related to me the story of how Hillary came to him and said, "I want to hire you to find the names, telephone numbers, and addresses of all the women that Bill is romancing, and when you get them, I want to make sure that you put the arm on these women so that they'll keep their mouths shut."

Then in the White House, Hillary continued this surveillance of Bill Clinton by creating a special squad of women in the White House led by Evelyn Lieberman, whose sole responsibility was to make sure that dangerous women—women who might talk—were kept away from Bill. In fact, when Monica Lewinsky started her liaison with Bill, Evelyn Lieberman knew about it and told Hillary.

It's fair to say that Edward Klein's information is secondhand. But there was a distinguished FBI agent, Gary Aldrich, who was assigned to the White House during this time. Gary Aldrich confirms the pattern of Hillary's intimate involvement in covering up Bill's philanderings, while at the same time cutting her some slack:

Hillary Clinton knew about Monica Lewinsky and the many other young women who were visiting Bill Clinton. Much of that activity was in the open. It's a small White House. There isn't much that can happen there without people seeing it.

I have to give Hillary Clinton some latitude, though, because even if you're the First Lady in a very public forum, you still have to process the feelings that would come with this sort of betrayal. So, I give her some flexibility on this.

That said, my biggest concern about Hillary Clinton is her conduct when things didn't go precisely her way. Whether it was an argument with Bill Clinton or something a staff member did, her furies were legendary. Word spread quickly around the White House about these blow-ups. And they weren't just once-in-a-while occasions. And we need to think about what this means.

Hillary's behavior under fire reminds me of an old saying in the FBI that when you have a pistol in your hand, you're supposed to aim and then fire, not fire and then aim. These kinds of emotional outbursts can cause subordinates to go off in the wrong direction to please the president. If they thought that Hillary Clinton was very angry about somebody, they would probably find a way to get rid of that person.

In Jeff Gerth and Don Van Natta Jr.'s book *Her Way: The Hopes and Ambitions of Hillary Rodham Clinton* (Little, Brown, 2007), they wrote that Hillary's defense activities ranged from the inspirational to the microscopic to the down and dirty. She received memos about the status of various press inquiries. She listened to a secretly recorded audio tape of a phone conversation of Clinton critics plotting their next attack. The tape contained discussions of another woman who might surface with allegations about her affair with Bill. Once again, Bill Clinton's chances were jeopardized by rumors of his womanizing. *Again,* it was up to Hillary to minimize the threats.

And in Carl Bernstein's book, *A Woman in Charge* (Knopf, 2007), he wrote that both Clintons went to great lengths to keep the lid on his infidelities, and that two partners of Hillary Clinton and the Rose Law Firm, Webb Hubbell and Vince Foster, were hired to represent women named in a lawsuit as having secret affairs with the governor. Hubbell and Foster questioned the women. And on one occasion Hillary Clinton was present for the questioning of the women Bill attacked. Isn't that a remarkable thing to contemplate?

Magazine editor R. Emmett Tyrrell has been a big Clinton nemesis for fifteen years. He has reported extensively on their record of using private investigators:

> This should, I think, worry a lot of people in the press and political life. I can't think of a political figure, certainly a political figure that's a candidate for president of the United States, who has such a record of using private investigators as Hillary. And by the way, this knowledge is not unique to me. Carl Bernstein mentions it in his book. I think Van Natta mentions it in his book.

Mark Levin, whose legal foundation for years kept the heat on the Clintons for their misdeeds, put it all in perspective. He says that when the Clintons play politics, well . . .

It's divide and conquer; it's brutalize; it's smear. They do the very things they say that they reject, which is the politics of personal destruction. That is her politics; that is his politics. They did everything they could to silence, for instance, their critics, including women who Clinton had abused throughout his governorship, and Hillary was involved in leading that effort.

We now know that she even listened to tapes of some conversations that were secretly recorded. I mean, you know, this is really stunning. And it's stunning to me how the media will give her a pass, and how the media pretends none of these things happen. And they accept the Hillary operatives' line, which is "that's old news."

Tyrrell discusses the same Clinton dodge:

One of her great claims throughout the 1990s and in her present career as senator is that she'll say, "Oh, that's old news." . . . Well, it's old news [only] because the Clintons are repeat offenders. They've been doing these things going right back to the 1980s. In writing my book on Bill in retirement, *The Clinton Crack-Up*, I made a discovery that I hadn't anticipated, and that was that all of the scandals that the Clintons found themselves enmeshed in, in the 1990s, all had precursors back in the 1980s.

Pardon-gate, they were guilty of their own little pardon-gate in 1981 when Clinton gave reckless pardons to people that almost sunk his career. . . . And tricky fund-raising problems that you saw in 1996 with Asian money, well, that went all the way back into the 1980s, 1986, when *The American Spectator* found they had the Indonesian-

Chinese money from the Lippo family, the Riady family coming in, and for that matter throughout the 1980s . . .

So the Clintons, there's nothing new about the Clintons, and even the fact that the press is forever waxing indignant about one scandal after another and then returning to hope renewed, this kind of cycle, I call it the cycle of the episodic apologists. . . . But then after the indignation exists for six or seven months, hope is renewed, and once again she is the next Eleanor Roosevelt.

| 4 |

CAN WE TRUST OUR NATION'S SECURITY TO THIS WOMAN?

Islamofascists have been waging war on America for almost thirty years, beginning with the 1979 sacking of our embassy in Tehran; continuing with the destruction of our Marine barracks in Beirut in 1983; the first bombing of the World Trade Center in 1993; a series of attacks on our embassies and ships during the Clinton administration; the three thousand lives lost on September 11, 2001; and numerous attempts since then to kill not only Americans but anyone who cherishes freedom.

The next president will be called upon to make difficult decisions; some we can anticipate, some we cannot. The man or woman who next assumes the mantle of leadership will be tested as perhaps none other before. Are we ready to trust this state of affairs to Hillary Clinton?

The participants in our film, who are quoted extensively in this book, looked back on the record of the Clintons in fighting terrorism in the 1990s and looked forward to what we could expect from Hillary should she win.

WHAT THE 1960s SHOULD HAVE
TAUGHT US ABOUT FIGHTING TERROR

An interesting perspective on our challenges past and future comes from terrorism authority and author of *Losing bin Laden* (Regnery, 2003), Richard Miniter:

> It is illustrative to look back on 1960s-era Los Angeles and New York. The liberal politicians of the time had reached this epiphany in thinking. They had discovered that criminal behavior was society's fault. In the enlightened liberal mind-set, it was society that had failed the underclass—practically forcing them into their evil ways.
>
> This mind-set led to an excessive concern for the criminal, at the expense of the victim. It led to laws and rules restricting local police, entangling them in bureaucracy, hampering their ability to make arrests and prosecute criminals. Predictably, the crime rate spiraled. Increases in the 500 percent range. Every measure of crime—from the petty to violent—increased.
>
> By the 1980s people said, "Enough is enough."
>
> In came Rudy Giuliani in New York and Daryl Gates in Los Angeles—they were law-and-order cops. They returned their respective cities to old-fashioned conservative policing. And within a few short years, we saw a dramatic decrease in crime—it actually dropped below 1965 levels. People could again stroll the streets of New York City at night without fear for their life. The L.A. gangs were effectively shut down and dispersed. We now had clear evidence of the best way to reduce crime. But some folks on the Left didn't want to learn the lesson.
>
> Indeed, in the 1990s we saw a similar distrust and skepticism about our intelligence services. Our FBI and CIA were being actively prohibited from doing their jobs. The Clinton administration imposed

all kinds of restrictions, not to mention gutting the budgets of these groups. So, just as the cop on the beat had not been able to arrest criminals without fear of prosecution himself, now our nation's spies faced untenable restrictions, which led ultimately to 9/11.

We're probably facing another twenty to thirty years of debate before the obvious parallel between fighting street thugs and fighting terrorists is made apparent to all. Or it may never become apparent— judging by the behavior of Democrats now that they again control the Congress. Liberals and civil libertarians may never see the value of fighting terrorism with every single weapon available to us. But the danger of waiting as long as we did on crime won't be the tens of thousands of innocent Americans murdered, but hundreds of thousands or even millions murdered.

We are all products of our formative years, shaped by the big events that swirled about us as we headed off to college or out on our own for the first time. And accordingly, says Richard Miniter, both Bill and Hillary Clinton are very much children of the sixties:

> The Clintons grew up with this intense suspicion of the use of American power, especially abroad. They didn't trust it, didn't like it. Then there was the worry of it backfiring, or some unintended consequence making things far worse.
>
> Instead, they preferred the law enforcement model: send the FBI overseas to conduct an investigation; use diplomatic pressure through the bureaucracy. Anything involving spooks in the dark, stealth at ten thousand feet, or submarines in the Indian Ocean made them nervous and uncomfortable.
>
> But there are problems in using the law enforcement model to fight terrorism.
>
> When the FBI is conducting a criminal investigation, they are

required to establish a chain of custody for any evidence they've obtained. In other words, they have to document who found an item and who all touched it at every turn until it arrives in the courtroom. If at any time they lose track of that evidence, then it becomes worthless. Even if it was unaccounted for five minutes time, theoretically it could have been tampered with and therefore not admissible as evidence. These rules make excellent sense in an advanced democracy like ours, but they are rather quaint when your investigators are sorting through an Arab or African city that's just been blasted by al-Qaeda bombs.

So by requiring a law enforcement response to terrorism, Clinton was sealing in failure. If Clinton had grasped the true horrific scope of the terrorist attacks, if he had not been distracted by Monica, if he had not been deeply suspicious of the use of U.S. military might—and this goes double for Hillary—then 9/11 might have been prevented, thousands of Americans dead might be alive today, and bin Laden might be a footnote instead of an ongoing threat.

Frank Gaffney calls upon his own firsthand experiences as a terrorism analyst and senior Pentagon official to assess the fundamental problem of viewing terrorism as a criminal act:

Each time terrorists struck on Clinton's watch, he regarded them as essentially criminals who needed to be dealt with in a law enforcement mode. There were exceptions. He would fire cruise missiles here and there. But there was no grand strategy, no real recognition of the character of the enemy we were confronting.

Understanding the true character of the enemy is crucial because it affects how you respond to them. If it's a law enforcement matter, you use law enforcement techniques, modalities, and personnel to try to contain the damage and prosecute the individuals involved. Such an approach is totally inappropriate, however, if—as I am firmly convinced—we are in a war for the free world and our very future as a free society.

Treating a global war with its potential for large-scale destruction as a law enforcement matter so dreadfully misconstrues the nature of the challenge as to condemn us to failure—failure to contain past damage, let alone to prevent what's coming next.

TRAGEDY OF MOGADISHU UNLEASHES THE TERRORIST GENIE

Few presidents get the conditions for governing that they want. Early on, they are confronted with events that shape their tenure, whether they like it or not. Early on in Bill Clinton's term, his own agenda was abruptly pushed aside by the incident we know as "Black Hawk Down" in Mogadishu, Somalia. Frank Gaffney provides a quick primer on Mogadishu:

> Events in Mogadishu began when the Bush administration responded to a serious humanitarian crisis by sending troops in to distribute food, provide medical relief, and assist in alleviating a desperate situation. By the time Clinton came in office, the humanitarian mission had devolved into chaos. Warlords and gangs were fighting among each other, and the people were caught in the middle.
>
> It was a difficult decision, made more difficult by our own actions. Bill Clinton's secretary of defense Les Aspin had been withholding shipments of equipment that were requested by commanders on the ground. That in turn contributed to vulnerabilities for our troops that were sent in harm's way, and those vulnerabilities were exploited by the warlords.
>
> All of this precipitated the now famous "Black Hawk Down" disaster in which we witnessed on prime-time television U.S. servicemen

being drug through the streets of Mogadishu. The American people were understandably repulsed and wanted action.

Bill and Hillary Clinton each reacted to the situation in Mogadishu in telling ways, says Richard Minter:

We know from associates of Hillary's that she considered Black Hawk Down a huge political embarrassment inherited from the Bush administration—never mind that the U.S. troops in Mogadishu had been noncombatant peacekeepers! She wanted the soldiers out immediately and made her feelings known to the president.

As for the president, we know that he spent the first moments afterward in a San Francisco hotel room using his special telephone to pull footage off of CNN. He wanted to see the downed helicopter and the damage that had been done to American troops.

He wasn't there ordering a military strike.

He wasn't there providing heavy armor for our troops.

He wanted to see exactly which images the U.S. media would show the American people. He was concerned how those images might affect his own popularity—nothing else.

Meanwhile, a man named bin Laden was also watching, and he, too, was concerned about his popularity. In bin Laden's mind and in his legend, he had defeated the Soviet Union in Afghanistan. Now he wanted to attack Americans and show that he alone in the world could defeat two superpowers.

So he challenged U.S. forces through proxies in Somalia; he financed a number of warlords there, supplying them with sophisticated weaponry and such. And in what al-Qaeda calls the battle of the Black Sea in Mogadishu, they lost eighty people, we lost nineteen, yet we retreated.

The lesson bin Laden drew from that was: the United States was an even weaker adversary than the Soviets, much more likely to run. It proved to be a very dangerous lesson to teach him.

GUTTING THE MILITARY AND INTELLIGENCE SERVICES

After the Mogadishu tragedy faded from the headlines, what did Bill Clinton do? He actually began proving to bin Laden that we were a weak adversary by beginning what Richard Miniter describes as unprecedented cuts in the military and intelligence budgets:

> You'd have to go back into the period immediately following World War I to see such a steep decline in U.S. military and intelligence spending.
>
> Now, the intelligence budget of the United States is a secret. No one knows the precise number except for the House and Senate Intelligence Committees. But in 1995, through a mistake in a court order, the number was revealed. And it was shocking because we learned that in 1995 the intelligence budget was 30 percent smaller than a decade earlier.
>
> The CIA and other intelligence agencies were being denied funds they needed to hire (1) analysts specializing in counterterrorism, (2) experts at interpreting satellite photographs, (3) translators who knew Arabic, Urdu, and other languages used by al-Qaeda.
>
> In the Reagan years, the counterterrorism desk at CIA was a red-hot ticket for your career. In the Clinton years, it was a graveyard, and everyone was either struggling to get out or just waiting for retirement. It was not considered a good career ticket to punch.
>
> What's extraordinary about this is that bin Laden emerged as a threat under Clinton's watch. . . . In 1993, we saw a number of attacks by al-Qaeda against Americans, including the [first] World Trade Center bombing and Mogadishu.

So the attacks against the United States were escalating at the same time Bill Clinton was cutting the military and intelligence budgets, and career CIA officers were realizing that if they wanted to fight al-Qaeda, they weren't going to advance in their careers.

So is it fair to tar Hillary with the same brush as Bill in the failures on the war on terror? Frank Gaffney reminds us:

> When Bill Clinton ran for office, he told us this was going to be a two-fer. You get Bill and Hillary—with all of her capabilities. There is a lot of evidence that she had a hand in deliberations that extended beyond healthcare.

A PROFOUND HOSTILITY TOWARD THE MILITARY

Certainly it is possible to excuse the Clintons for their overreaction to the Black Hawk Down incident. They didn't know bin Laden was watching. The American people were in fact sickened by the images, and many were happy to see U.S. troops pull out. So in seeking a broader measure of performance in fighting terror, Frank Gaffney looks at the Clintons' impact on military readiness, morale, and national security over time:

> A very interesting and I think insightful moment occurred early in the Clinton presidency when a White House staffer addressed a general who was coming to the White House complex. With a degree of contempt that was palpable, the staffer said, "I don't talk to the military."
>
> The Clinton administration believed the threats our nation had previously faced were no more, and that we could balance the budget largely by gutting spending on the military. Sure enough, the budget was balanced, but at a huge cost in terms of day-to-day readiness of

the United States Armed Forces and in their ability to be prepared for tomorrow's wars.

As we look back on the Clinton years, there was hostility toward those in uniform. The Clinton presidency affected troop morale and readiness, and set the stage for problems that continue to affect us today.

So when Senator Clinton is seen being critical of the Bush administration for not making our military ready, that's the pot calling the kettle black. Secretary of Defense Donald Rumsfeld came in for a lot of ridicule for talking seemingly cavalierly about how you fight wars with the military you have, not the military you would like to have. Unfortunately, Mr. Rumsfeld had to fight with the military bequeathed by Mr. Clinton.

Congressman John Mica recalls how the Clintons treated the military:

I will never forget witnessing the disrespect they showed the military at White House receptions. They treated the military like lowly servants. We had enemies who had publicly declared war on us, and yet the Clintons couldn't be bothered with the men and women of our military. I saw no real difference between Bill and Hillary in their contempt for all matters military.

Congressman Dan Burton has similar recollections:

Let's begin back at the first attack on the World Trade Center. What did Clinton do about that? Nothing.

There were numerous attacks on Americans around the world. What did Clinton do about those attacks? Well, he bombed an aspirin factory in Africa to make it look like he was doing something. Other than that?

He slashed funding for the CIA and our intelligence gathering capability. He made it impossible for the CIA and the FBI to work together. Had these two agencies been allowed to work together, we might have been able to prevent 9/11.

So from all of this history, I don't see how we could expect any different responses in a third Clinton term.

While Washington insiders bring one view to the conduct of national security matters, the folks in the field often bring a different view. We asked Clare Lopez, who spent twenty years as a field operative for the CIA, to talk about the effects of the Clinton budget cuts on U.S. military and intelligence operations. As someone who worked domestically and abroad in Central/South America, Africa, and the Balkans, Clare Lopez brings a frontline view:

During the Clinton years of the 1990s, we saw a slow retreat from the aggressive get-the-job-done attitude that I had seen earlier. I would see a lack of willingness to take risks, a gun-shyness, a new concentration on working only with people who were known to be of fine moral fiber.

Yet if there is any constant in my old line of work, it is that you get the best intel from the less savory characters you ferret out of dirty backwater holes. You don't get actionable intel from talking to a Ministry head. But the rules came down that we couldn't meet with anyone who wasn't a choirboy or Boy Scout. I thought this detrimental to our mission.

I'm speaking specifically of a new set of rules Clinton handed us, which were known as the Deutch guidelines. Basically, these guidelines restricted how the mission could be carried out. They required a tighter vetting of sources. They forbade us from paying anyone who had a police record. The Deutch guidelines inhibited intelligence collection—on that point there is no disagreement.

We also saw the closing of a number of CIA stations and a drastic cutback in the number of officers serving. As a result, in the post 9/11 world, we find ourselves scrambling to rebuild the services.

It takes three to five years for new hires, whether a case officer or an analyst, to become familiar with the work and understand the regions they've been assigned to. So the cutbacks of the mid-90s were detrimental then, even more so now. We are desperate for officers who know the Middle East, who know terrorism, who know weapons of mass destruction. Without these assets, we are laboring at a distinct disadvantage.

In regard to our relative advantages in the war on terror, I am often asked how much our enemies know about the shortcomings in our intelligence community. I can say unequivocally, they know a lot. Our enemies in the global war on terror are exquisitely aware of the culture of the United States, the status of our intelligence services, the abilities we have to counter their activities. I'm afraid they are much more aware of our capabilities than we are of theirs.

PUTTING CIVIL LIBERTIES BEFORE NATIONAL SECURITY

While the CIA was being actively hamstrung in their activities by new rules out of Washington, the FBI was facing similar restrictions on the homeland. Veteran security analyst Michael Ledeen wrote that "Clinton prevented the Justice Department from acting on the information it had and blocked its efforts to strike a meaningful blow against terror. . . ."

It was a classic case of trying to do good things and ending up doing very bad things. There was a mind-set in the Clinton Justice Department that people being investigated by grand juries needed some protections—to guard against a police state. A worthy goal.

So the rules were written to keep any evidence introduced in a grand jury testimony locked up, compartmentalized. That way, nobody else could to see it and trample on someone's rights. But then that mind-set was applied to FBI investigations because the FBI is in the business of prosecuting criminals.

To make this happen, the Clinton administration created a "wall" between the FBI and the rest of the intelligence community. So in the case of the first World Trade Center bombing, for example, all of the data that the FBI compiled was kept "walled off" from the rest of the intelligence community. CIA never got to see it; NSA never got to see it. That data was not available for use in international terrorist investigations and counterterrorism operations.

Eventually we all learned of these rules when the 9/11 Commission Report shined a light on them. Through the commission, we learned that the CIA could not be faulted for saying, "You know, if we had known that the blind sheikh in prison in New York was making phone calls to the people who later participated in terrorist events, we could have stopped them." That could have stopped them, possibly. But the Clinton administration was more interested in our civil liberties than our national security.

Long before the 9/11 Commission, there were many other similar commissions, and they all concluding the same two things: we're not ready for a terrorist attack, and we have much to do if we want to be ready. But report after report, nobody was inclined to do anything. Why, you may ask?

Presidents have invariably found the whole subject of counterterrorism very off-putting because they are asked to make difficult, dangerous decisions that could easily fail. So there is always a big political price to be paid. Therefore, president after president has kicked that particular tin can on down the road, leaving it to his successor and hoping that nothing happens on his watch.

So Bill Clinton was not the only president to err on the terrorism front, says Michael Ledeen, but he was unique among modern presidents for his lack of interest in intel:

> Case in point: Director of Central Intelligence James Woolsey only had two real meetings with the president in his two years as director. Things were so bad that when this crazy guy crash-landed a plane on the back lawn of the White House one day, the joke around town was, "It must have been Woolsey still trying to get a meeting with the president!"
>
> The thing is, the intel business exists for one consumer—the president. And like any other business, it's a two-way street. If your customer keeps asking you questions, keeps tasking you to do more, you perform better. But Clinton almost never asked for any intel, and the intel business felt demoralized. And since Bill and Hillary's term is universally described as a copresidency, we have to presume that she was part of that problem.

Hillary has said repeatedly in interviews that if her husband had been shown a classified report titled "Bin Laden determined to attack inside the United States," he would taken it more seriously than President Bush has. To which Congressman John Mica replies:

> Hillary can say whatever she likes. But there is no doubt Clinton had a great deal of information about bin Laden, and that several attempts to go after bin Laden were bungled.
>
> As for Bush, he did not even have his cabinet in place by 9/11. The election outcome was slow in being decided by the Supreme Court. On 9/11, Bush was still facing Senate confirmation issues. After 9/11, to hear his critics, Bush has been too aggressive!
>
> If you look at the policy decision that most impacted 9/11, it was

the so-called "firewall" that was placed between the Department of Justice, the FBI, and the CIA. So even if one agency had information on bin Laden, they couldn't share it with another agency. That was the law Bill Clinton *did* lay down—a law Hillary can try to run from, but can't hide from.

Washington reporter Amanda Carpenter adds that the 9/11 Commission Report also speaks to the role Hillary played in going after bin Laden:

There is one passage in the *9/11 Commission Report*, in chapter 4, that deals directly with Hillary Clinton's impact on our ability to get Osama bin Laden. There was a time when the intel was so good, we knew where Osama bin Laden was sleeping. We had some Afghani tribals on board, ready to go in and take out bin Laden. They had practiced the mission. But there was a problem.

These tribals wanted to be paid for their efforts—not an unusual request. But there was a concern that the First Lady might object to paying these people, because it might reflect negatively on her ability to work with women. See, the Afghani tribals didn't have a very good record of human rights. So the mission was scotched—solely out of fear of upsetting Hillary.

And from the author of *Losing bin Laden,* Richard Miniter:

At the time, I talked to President Clinton's national security advisor, Tony Lake. He told me on the record that he was first briefed about the threat posed by bin Laden by early 1994. That's bin Laden by name. The terrorist organization al-Qaeda was known as early as December 1992 when CIA cables from Yemen identified them. It then took them about a year and a half to figure out who bin Laden was.

Some Arab intelligence services said he was a "moving bank," simply a financier of terrorism. But by 1993, the first year of the Clinton administration, it became clear that bin Laden wasn't just a financier, but an attacker, in fact one who specialized in attacking Americans. Indeed, al-Qaeda's attacks increased in number and lethality every year of the Clinton administration.

August 7, 1998, two U.S. embassies, one in Kenya and other in Tanzania, exploded from car bombs put forward by al-Qaeda. More than a dozen Americans were dead, and hundreds of Africans. President Clinton had to respond. It took him days to even decide, perhaps because this was also the time of the Monica Lewinsky investigation.

Clinton found himself alternating between his personal fate and the fate of the nation. The bombings were August 7; he didn't strike until August 20. He lobbed some cruise missiles. I have been to the wreckage of the factories in Khartoum and the places in Afghanistan where those cruise missiles landed. Those missiles had pinpoint accuracy, which I could see. But I could also see the error in U.S. policy.

Clinton simply lobbed cruise missiles. There were no follow-up strikes, no attempt to destroy the organization as a whole or to end its ability to strike Americans.

Here we had two U.S. embassies destroyed, an act of war by any definition, and yet Bill Clinton responded only with a punitive strike, and a temporary one at that.

Now in fairness to Bill Clinton, he didn't have any specific warning that terrorists were going to strike a specific place at a specific time, just as George Bush hasn't had any specific warning. There's always a lot of chatter in the channels about potential terrorist activity, but nobody's ever phoned ahead. That's why the president's approach to terrorism is so important.

During the Clinton years, there was a regular stream of intelligence coming into the CIA, and into the White House, about al-Qaeda's evil designs. Every single year, al-Qaeda either killed or tried to kill Americans.

Bin Laden declared war on the United States openly eight times between 1996 and 1998.

Bin Laden didn't say, "We don't like you very much." He made a declaration of war.

Bin Laden said that he intended to destroy the United States and to convert the survivors of the war to Islam forcibly.

Bin Laden's words were very clear, very specific.

And bin Laden backed up his words with a continuous trail of blood.

So while Clinton never had a specific warning, he had an opportunity and an obligation to act before bin Laden dug himself deep into the mountains, making the task of finding of him increasingly difficult.

Frank Gaffney corroborates these conclusions:

The challenge in gathering wartime intelligence is sifting the "signal" from the "noise." The signal is always there. It's a question of stripping out the noise and trying to connect the dots. And it's fair to say that throughout the Clinton years, there were plenty of dots to connect.

EARLY AL-QAEDA PLOTS TO KILL
THOUSANDS OF AMERICANS

One of the earliest briefings given to Clinton by his national security aides came early on, in 1994, as recalled by Richard Miniter:

Operation Bojinka, which in Servo-Croat means "loud bang," was an al-Qaeda operation in the Philippines in 1994. Al-Qaeda had been extending its tentacles in the Philippines since the early 1990s—they were recruiting there; they had training camps in the jungles. Khalid Sheikh Mohammed, the planner of the 9/11 attacks, set up a cell operation outside of Manila (in part because he was interested in an attractive Philippine dentist nearby). Also involved was Ramzi Yousef, who had masterminded the 1993 World Trade Center bombing.

These guys weren't in the Philippines on vacation—though they had trimmed their beards and went to strip clubs to try to appear inconspicuous to the outside world. But in a small apartment, they began cooking explosives, and they had three different plots in mind. . . .

One plot was to assassinate President Clinton when he visited the Philippines in 1994.

The second plot was to kill the pope, who was visiting the Philippines that year. Most ominously, when police raided the apartment, they found a message on the answering machine from a Catholic uniform service saying, "Your bishop cassock is ready." The terrorists' plan was to dress like a Catholic monsignor, with a bomb underneath the black robe, and while kneeling to kiss the pope's ring, detonating the bomb.

The third plot was to simultaneously blow up eleven airplanes bound for the United States over the Pacific, potentially killing three thousand people. The plot was simple:

They would pick flights with a stopover in the middle.

Each of the eleven terrorists would get on the first leg of the flight, carrying what looked like contact lens solutions and a Timex watch.

Once the flight was airborne, the terrorist would go into the bathroom, take out the solutions, and pour one into the other.

These two colorless, odorless liquids would merge to form nitroglycerin jelly.

Then he would take a small wire, maybe even a paperclip, and jam it into the Timex watch, set the alarm, and stick the other end of the wire into the nitroglycerin jelly.

Then he would put this bomb into a sandwich bag and leave it under his seat as he departed the plane on the first leg.

On the second leg of the flight, the alarm would ring—sending an electric signal down the wire into the glob of nitroglycerin jelly, blowing the plane in half.

Ramzi Yousef actually succeeded once, on a test flight from Cebu City stopping in Manila on the way to Tokyo. Luckily for most of the passengers onboard, he didn't use enough explosive. He did blow a hole in the plane and killed an innocent Japanese engineer. But the aircraft was able to make an emergency landing in Okinawa.

In the minds of Ramzi Yousef and Khalid Sheikh Mohammed, however, they had proved that they could get bomb-making material onto a plane, they could construct the bomb in the bathroom, they could safely exit the plane, and on the second leg of the flight the bomb could detonate. Now all they needed to do was expand onto a larger scale, and that was Operation Bojinka.

Eleven airplanes would explode over the Pacific within a half hour of each other, killing upward of three thousand Americans—a deadlier day than even 9/11.

Bill Clinton was fully briefed on all this.

ON HER OWN AS SENATOR, CONCERNED ABOUT TERRORISM?

Once Bill Clinton had served his term and the task of fighting the war on terror fell to George Bush, Hillary moved to New York and got herself elected to the Senate. She was on her own now. So how concerned was she about terrorism? *New York Times* investigative reporter Jeff Gerth did some digging:

Hillary came into the Senate in January 2001. She put out a press release to her constituents boasting of how proud she was to get onto the Health Committee, Environment and Public Works Committee, and Budget Committee—all dealing with the social domestic issues that have interested her for many years. She did not get onto any committees that dealt with national security, military matters, or terrorism. She wasn't interested in those issues.

Indeed, we went through over two hundred speeches that were posted on her Web site prior to 9/11, and there was not a single speech on counterterrorism or threats to the homeland. Then, of course, 9/11 hit, and she rushed onto the *CBS Evening News*, and when Dan Rather asked her about 9/11, she said, "I've always been very concerned about the threat of terrorism—I consider that our number one homeland threat."

It was an odd answer given her lack of engagement previously.

Former Speaker of the House Newt Gingrich gives Hillary somewhat higher marks for waking up to the terrorist threat:

After 9/11 she got herself onto the Armed Services Committee. Even though it doesn't make conservatives happy, many professional military people think she's a serious, hardworking person who has done her job pretty well.

Terrorism expert Frank Gaffney also seeks to be fair in assessing Hillary's record and her position statements on the war on terror:

Senator Clinton has used the same language Republicans and some Democrats have used to characterize the war on terror. She has talked about the need to improve homeland security. She did get onto the Senate Armed Services Committee.

But as far as I know, she has not discussed with any certainty that we are at war with a totalitarian ideology that exists not only abroad but here in the United States as well, and how that ideology is systematically working to destroy us. I would think that's the kind of clarity and forceful exposition we should expect from anyone who purports to be a viable, let alone successful, candidate for the presidency of the United States.

Giving Senator Clinton the benefit of the doubt, she was genuinely surprised by what happened on 9/11, as were most Americans. You could view her voting record and position statements in the months following 9/11 as considerably more robust than many of her party.

However, the further we've gotten away from 9/11, the more she has taken positions favored by the extreme left of her party. This suggests that whatever Mrs. Clinton took away from 9/11 is now slipping away. Or perhaps she never meant it in the first place, and she is simply reverting to form.

Longtime Washington observer Bob Novak sees Hillary as the consummate politician, casting her votes in line with the latest poll results. Bob Novak is concerned that we don't know what Hillary *really* believes:

People should be concerned if they do not know where Senator Clinton really stands. Look, when Bill Clinton ran for president in 1992, he never made clear whether he supported the Gulf War of 1991. Not being a senator, he didn't have to be on record. His subsequent conduct in the war against terrorism was a reflection of how little we knew about his real positions on foreign and military policy.

Terrorism expert Richard Miniter sums up Hillary's capacity to serve and the questions she should be answering in this election:

America is at war, in a battle to the death. It's al-Qaeda or it's us; it's freedom or it's slavery; it's really that simple.

Is Hillary Clinton someone who seems fully committed to winning the war, to banishing this scourge of terror from our lives? Is she really that person?

Or is she someone like her husband, who considers every crisis something to be bargained with, who doesn't understand the difference between politics as usual and a nation at war?

Does Hillary Clinton really have the strength of character, the quality of mind, the doggedness to keep going through the slough of despond and get to victory? Is she Churchill? Is she FDR?

Or is she simply a timeserver?

When politicians are running for office, they tend to speak in grand sweeping declarations that offend no one and can warm even a cynic's heart. Speechwriters call it the "cotton candy" in the speech. Hillary's speeches are no different, so how do we find out what she really believes? In the area of national security, we look at her votes on the Patriot Act and wiretapping. Those are contentious issues for liberals and conservatives alike, and they tell us where Hillary's priorities lie in the war against terror.

THE PATRIOT ACT—TAKING TERRORISM SERIOUSLY

Richard Miniter tells a story about the Patriot Act in action:

March 2002, Islamabad, Pakistan. Khalid Sheik Mohammed, the operational planner of the 9/11 attacks, is captured at gunpoint. On his person are two cell phones and a laptop computer. The National Security Agency and CIA together exploit these devices and discover within a few days that thousands of phone numbers have been called by Khalid Sheikh Mohammed around the world. But here's the frightening part: hundreds of those phone numbers were inside the United States.

Now, imagine you are the National Security Adviser and you walk into the Oval Office to brief the president. And you say, "Hundreds of people inside the United States are talking to the number three guy in al-Qaeda—should we listen in on those calls?"

If you are Hillary Clinton, your answer is no.

National Review's Washington editor Kate O'Beirne adds another dimension to the question of leadership in a time of terror:

We are involved in shooting wars in Afghanistan and Iraq against determined enemies. We face enormous security challenges at home that mandate policies and legislation such as the Patriot Act to give our law enforcement officers the tools they need to protect Americans. To have a President Hillary Clinton and a Speaker Nancy Pelosi who do not support these kinds of tough security measures could be, at a time like this, extremely perilous.

Frank Gaffney recognizes that it's extremely difficult to project how someone might act once in the hot seat of the presidency—and that goes double for Hillary:

We don't know what a President Hillary Clinton might do when the decision is hers and hers alone. But one can reasonably extrapolate from her public policy statements that she would not prosecute a war for the free world aggressively using all of the instruments at her disposal. She would not be willing to offend her friends on the Left who worry excessively about infringements on civil liberties.

So, would she support a Patriot Act in the future? I tend to think not. What is her position on warrantless wiretapping? She has been opposed to it. Will she support aggressive techniques for incarcerating and interrogating people who are engaged in terrorist actions against us? I tend to think not.

Again, setting aside the charm offensive she launched on the military post 9/11, the Hillary Clinton of the future will likely be the Hillary Clinton of the past—a politician of the Left—and I don't think that's good for the security of the United States.

CIA analyst Clare Lopez speaks to the price we'd pay if the Patriot Act was rolled back:

The degradation of our intelligence capabilities during the Clinton years affected our national technological capability. And although we're trying very hard now, under the Patriot Act, to reconstitute our national technological capability, there's a great deal of catching up to do. An enormous investment has to be made.

If, as Senator Clinton has suggested, measures of the Patriot Act were thrown out, I'm afraid the United States would be set back at a great disadvantage in the war on terror. Here is why:

This is a global war, and so are the forces involved. When they make telephone calls, when they use cell phones, when they use the Internet, we need to have the means to find that out, to monitor that, and to take steps to counter it. That is what the Patriot Act allows.

If it is repealed, we will be thrown back to the time when we had a huge disadvantage against terrorists, a time when we couldn't even monitor their phone calls without first going out and getting a court order, a time that resulted in 9/11.

When Senator Clinton says that if her husband had known that terrorists were planning to run airplanes into the World Trade Center, he would have done something about it, I'm sure he would have. It's precisely this ability to know far enough ahead of time what the jihadis are planning to do—that is what the Patriot Act helps enable.

IT'S A QUESTION OF EMOTIONAL STABILITY

When all is said and done come election day, and voters go to perform their solemn duty, the outcome may well come down to one question: do we want Hillary's finger on the button? As the senior FBI agent in the White House under the Clintons, Gary Aldrich talks about his experiences with Hillary, and his thoughts about her as commander in chief:

> I've been privileged to meet a number of presidents and observe them up close in their daily activities. And the one thing that stands out about our better presidents is their calm personality, their ability to handle adversity in a graceful way. My fear about Hillary Clinton is that we would see these emotional outbursts, this over-the-top behavior.
>
> Her emotional reactions, her furies, her blow-ups—these aren't just once-in-a-while occasions. They seem to be a constant issue. She seems unable to process information that is contrary to her own mind-set or to deal with it in any kind of graceful way.

Michael Medved, the popular radio talk show host, has known Hillary since their days together at Yale Law School. He has a different take on her emotional qualifications:

> Personally, I think there's a real chance that Hillary would try to be a Margaret Thatcher. It was striking to watch her in a recent debate mixing it up with John Edwards. She's manlier than John Edwards—I mean that in a good sense, not insulting. I thought she looked terrific. She doesn't always look good on camera, but in that moment

she had more cojones than John Edwards. But then, there are sea slugs for whom that might be true. Point is, Hillary might be very eager, even too eager, to demonstrate her toughness if elected.

On the other hand, I think our enemies look on this election differently. I think they would view the election of Hillary as the ultimate confirmation that American society has lost its manhood, has gone completely squishy and feminine.

THREE (OF MANY) DESPERATE ATTEMPTS TO COVER UP BLUNDERS

A very accomplished filmmaker named Cyrus Nowrasteh has written and directed a number of films including *The Day Reagan Was Shot* and TV shows including *La Femme Nikita, DEA,* and *Falcon Crest.* Most recently he wrote and produced the miniseries *The Path to 9/11,* which aired on ABC in September 2006. It was a huge ratings smash, finishing second in the ratings behind the football game. But it almost didn't air. In the lead-up to the broadcast, there was a massive campaign to discredit and censor the movie. There has never been an attack on a movie so broad or vicious, as Cyrus Nowrasteh recalls none too fondly:

> It was all political spin generated by ex-President Clinton from his offices in Harlem, where he met with left-wing bloggers to discuss how they could get *The Path to 9/11* pulled from the air.
>
> They shut down ABC's e-mail system and phone system. I got hate mail and death threats. They set out to destroy us. The intimidation campaign included five U.S. senators led by Harry Reid sending a letter to Disney/ABC threatening to revoke their station licenses if they didn't pull or recut the movie.
>
> Now you've got to understand, the people coordinating these campaigns had not seen the movie. They freely admitted it. The whole

thing was a coordinated political spin campaign to protect Bill Clinton's legacy.

I got hate mail. I even got hate faxes. And all the phones at my house just started ringing—the house line, my office line, my children's lines. I'd pick up the phone and say hello, as one usually does, and on the other end I heard things like, "I hope you die" or "How dare you release these lies."

I learned that all my home numbers and address had been released on the Internet by left-wing bloggers. One of the postings onto the Internet said, "The gloves are off, accidents occur." So we changed our voice mail message, stopped answering calls that we didn't recognize on Caller I.D., and called the police in.

I got a follow-up phone call from the FBI telling me that the Internet posting qualified as a death threat. I never really believed, frankly, that I was in danger. I felt that a lot of these guys on the Internet are just nuts, and very courageous behind their keyboards. I also have a very big German shepherd. But it's unsettling, because you don't know.

To corroborate Cyrus Nowrasteh's claim that Bill Clinton orchestrated this entire campaign of hateful censorship, we found that the accomplished author Carol Felsenthal is writing a book about Bill Clinton's activities since leaving the White House—to be published in early 2008. Ms. Felsenthal has interviewed Sandy Berger and many of the bloggers involved in this campaign. She will reveal in her book what she learned about the meeting that took place in Harlem at President Clinton's offices.

As a result of the intimidation campaign, Disney/ABC chose to delete about three minutes from the five-hour miniseries. In our film, we showed the deleted sequence, and Cyrus Nowrasteh provided commentary:

They forced me to cut a sequence set in Afghanistan. In it CIA operatives are coordinating with Afghan tribals to try and capture or kill bin Laden. They have bin Laden's compound surrounded. They know where he is. All they need to do is coordinate with Washington. So they get on the satellite phone with Sandy Berger, Richard Clarke, and George Tenet in Washington to get the final green light to go ahead with this operation.

This is the sequence they were most upset about. President Clinton claims it never happened; they never got that close to bin Laden; they never had such an opportunity; it just never occurred. These are Bill Clinton's words.

So, was this sequence accurate? Did it really happen? I am asked all the time, "How true is it?" Let the experts respond to that:

Michael Scheuer, head of the Counterterrorist Center at the CIA at the time, sent an e-mail to ABC saying the core of the movie was irrefutably true. There were at least ten such opportunities to capture or kill bin Laden. In fact, Michael Scheuer has since gone on television and called President Clinton and Sandy Berger outright liars.

Buzz Patterson, chief military aide to President Clinton at the time, says he witnessed at least five such instances in which Sandy Berger or the president killed operations in progress.

Steven Emerson, of the Investigative Project on Terrorism, came forward after the broadcast aired and said *The Path to 9/11* is 100 percent accurate.

Gary Schroen, CIA officer and first American into Afghanistan after 9/11, has attested to the veracity of the movie.

These aren't politicians; these aren't spinners; these aren't bloggers. These are people who either were there or who are experts on the subject. *The Path to 9/11* got it right. That's why they were upset. We exposed the hot-button truth that they'd been trying to bury for years.

When Sandy Berger went to the National Archives in 2003 and

stole the documents relating to this sequence in Afghanistan, the jig was up. The documents Berger stole pertained to the sequence in my film *The Path to 9/11*. They are criminally guilty of distorting history.

Cyrus Nowrasteh's film *was* released in its entirety at the Liberty Film Festival. Sitting in the audience was Frank Gaffney, assistant secretary of defense under President Reagan and current head of the Center for Security Policy. After watching the film, Frank Gaffney sees why the Clintons are so nervous:

The deleted scene in *Path to 9/11* looked at the very memos relating to that scotched raid in Afghanistan. So when Sandy Berger removed all copies of those memos from the national archives illegally, stuffing them in his socks and then cutting them up with scissors, it appeared that they had something terribly damaging to cover up.

The guilt that Bill Clinton has for his past mistakes is telling, but does it weigh on the presidential ambitions of his wife? Cyrus Nowrasteh suggests that the entire hateful censorship campaign may have been more about her than him:

Disney/ABC was scheduled to release the DVD version of *The Path to 9/11* in January 2007. But January came and went, and no DVD. I followed up with Mark Pedowitz, a high-level exec at ABC (now president of Touchstone TV). He told me he didn't know when the DVD would be released. When I asked why, he said, "If Hillary weren't running for president, this wouldn't be a problem." And I told him that he was making an argument for releasing it sooner, before the heat of the campaign season. He just looked at me and kind of smiled. That's where it ended.

Clearly with Hillary running for the White House, they don't want terrorism as an issue. I think they feel vulnerable on it.

As a radio host, Mark Levin naturally is concerned about censorship:

The effort by the Clintons to censor *The Path to 9/11* is more evidence of where these people are coming from. That conduct was so un-American and so repulsive, and yet the Democrats in the Senate joined with them and wrote a letter that was basically threatening to ABC television, basically warning them about their licenses, warning them about their right to actually broadcast.

As for the content of *The Path to 9/11,* the official portrayed, Sandy Berger, certainly acted like a man with a guilty conscience. Sandy Berger's theft from the National Archives ruined his reputation and set a new low for outrageous behavior by public officials. Berger not only stole classified documents, but he did it so foolishly that some have even speculated that he was purposely trying to focus attention on the foolishness of his actions to deflect attention from the gravity of his crime.

We asked several people to comment on this bizarre episode, including Buzz Patterson—the military aide who was there with Clinton:

Sandy Berger is a very intelligent guy. He would not risk his reputation and law practice and a potentially lengthy jail term if there wasn't something damaging in the National Archives. So why did he go in, steal documents, and shred them?

There's no doubt in my mind that Berger destroyed the paper trail that pointed to what President Clinton knew in the days leading up to 9/11. Destroying those documents was felony number one. He wouldn't do that without guidance from Bill Clinton, and that's felony number two. Berger knew there was a smoking gun.

Berger knew the 9/11 Commission would be reviewing those documents and they would find something terribly damaging.

Also close to the action was Richard Miniter, author of *Losing bin Laden* and editorial page writer for the *Wall Street Journal Europe*:

Sandy Berger's theft from the National Archives wasn't exactly the Kennedy assassination, was it? But it was significant because we need to study both the Clinton years and Bush years as dueling approaches to terrorism to see what works best for the good of the country.

When you destroy the historical record, you destroy the ability to learn from the past. As costly as Bill Clinton's mistakes against al-Qaeda were, they were also invaluable in instructing our movement forward—both in terms of what to do and what not to do.

I have interviewed Sandy Berger a number of times. He went into the National Archives and located what's known as the Millennium After-Action Review. Here's context on that review document:

Richard Clarke, then counterterrorism czar in the White House, was made aware by sources in Jordan that al-Qaeda was planning a series of spectacular attacks on U.S. soil on the eve of the millennium. Clarke put together a "war room" with the blessing of Sandy Berger and Bill Clinton, overriding all the bureaucratic rules and restrictions to stop any al-Qaeda effort to kill Americans. Every dimension of American power and authority was brought to bear against al-Qaeda. And as a result, there were no attacks by al-Qaeda anywhere on Millennium Eve.

It was a tremendous success!

Afterward, the question for President Clinton was: do we continue on this war footing—actively trying to disrupt al-Qaeda, or do we go back to the status quo—letting all the bureaucratic restrictions return?

That was the question facing the Clinton administration in the months before the 9/11 attacks. So, how did they deal with that question?

The answer could be found in the Millennium After-Action Review—a loose-leaf binder about two inches thick, of which there were thirteen copies made. Now some Clinton partisans will contend that Sandy Berger didn't destroy anything because there were copies of all the documents he destroyed. This is true, but misleading. We have numerous copies of the report, but we no longer have President Clinton's copy. And that's important because Clinton made notes in the margins of the report.

Should we make the CIA and FBI work closer together? Clinton might have written in the margin: no.

Should we share intelligence and law enforcement? Clinton might have written: no.

Should we wiretap suspects inside the United States without a warrant? What did Clinton write?

Only Clinton and Sandy Berger know what he wrote, because it is Clinton's copy that he destroyed.

Now Sandy Berger is an intelligent man. He would not have destroyed those documents unless there was something very damaging in them that the 9/11 Commission members were about to find. So what was he trying to hide, and who was he trying to protect?

Certainly Bill Clinton was one beneficiary of his crimes. Isn't Hillary Clinton the other?

Congressmen John Mica and Dan Burton were charged with investigating Sandy Berger's theft of classified documents. But they met roadblock after roadblock—typical of all Clinton investigations. Plus, in this case senior officials at the National Archives and the Department of Justice made plenty of mistakes in their handling of the matter, so those officials have been less than eager to press forward with investigations. This case may reopen at some future time when Democrats are not in the position to squelch the truth. But for now the Clintons have accomplished their aims, says John Mica:

> Sandy Berger had a sincere interest in foreign policy, but that interest was viewed through the lens of getting Bill Clinton reelected and preserving Clinton's legacy and the Democratic Party's hold on the presidency. So he went into the National Archives, destroyed key documents, and was found guilty of felony activity and convicted for his actions. Basically, he was altering history, cleansing history.
>
> To steal the most highly classified documents in government, destroy them, admit to that act, be convicted for it, and then basically get a slap on the hand? It was a travesty!
>
> I do not know the personal relationship that Sandy Berger continues to have with Hillary Clinton. But look, he doesn't have to do another thing. He has already provided them with the gift that keeps on giving. He has cleansed history for them. He has made Bill Clinton look good, or at least neutral, on 9/11, and by that action, he has also given Hillary an opportunity to move forward. He did his deed.
>
> What would have happened if the public was to learn that Bill Clinton's inaction brought on 9/11?
>
> Hillary Clinton would be cooked goose.
>
> Sandy Berger had a mission, and that mission was to go in and clean up history, clean up mistakes, destroy any evidence of error or culpability. He accomplished that.

Now, amazingly, this same Sandy Berger who admitted to stealing these secret papers is once again an advisor to Hillary Clinton. Indeed, he is one of three people who are leading the team of foreign policy advisors for her campaign. And it makes one wonder which is more important to her: national security or her own political skin?

If there's any real question about the Clintons' sensitivity on the issue of terrorism, the answer lies in a TV interview Bill Clinton gave recently. As Amanda Carpenter recalls:

> A clear sign that the Clintons are sensitive about their credibility on military issues was revealed in the interview Bill Clinton did with FOX News' Chris Wallace recently. The interview had been going fine. Chris Wallace had been lobbing the former president softball questions. Then at about eight minutes into the interview, Wallace asked, "Mr. Clinton, do you think you did enough to get Osama bin Laden?" All of a sudden, Clinton got red in the face. He cut off the interview. He leaned menacingly over Wallace and jabbed his finger in Wallace's face. Now why would such a straightforward question upset Bill Clinton so much?
>
> Look at the *9/11 Commission Report*, chapter 4. You'll learn that we had bin Laden in our sights. Our intelligence had tracked him to a place called Tarnak Farm in Afghanistan. We were ready to pull a trigger. Bin Laden would have been done. But it didn't happen. . . .
>
> Why didn't Clinton act when he had the chance? We don't know for sure. We may never know for sure—because the record of the event was destroyed illegally by Sandy Berger. Clearly the Clinton administration made such a terrible mistake in the war on terror that they risked their reputations and very dignity to destroy the evidence.

THE COMMANDER IN CHIEF SLEEPING
WITH THE LOBBYIST IN CHIEF?

In this war on terror, America is most vulnerable at our seaports. Huge cargo containers come in by the thousands, making any attempt to monitor and control what's in those containers very difficult. For this reason, headlines were made in February 2006 when a company named Dubai Ports World was found to be competing to operate U.S. ports.

Dubai Ports World is owned by the country of Dubai, which doesn't allow workers to unionize, doesn't allow women the most basic of rights, doesn't allow Jews to enter, and doesn't try to stop known terrorists from operating from within its borders. Dubai's top lobbyist in America is a man named Bill Clinton. And having Mr. Clinton as your lobbyist would seem to offer some advantage should Hillary become president. It might also create a conflict of interest.

While voting on the ports deal, Hillary claimed to have no idea her husband was involved with Dubai Ports World. Bob Novak speaks to the credibility and style of Hillary Clinton:

> She simply does not give straight answers to questions. No matter who is asking. For example, the first debate in this presidential cycle was emceed by George Stephanopoulos, who had been her aide in the White House. She would not answer even his questions! Ask her any question and she doesn't know anything. She doesn't know how the documents got lost in Whitewater. She doesn't know how her law firm billing records got lost. She doesn't know her husband works for Dubai Ports. That's her modus operandi.
>
> Bill Clinton is a popular figure—a likeable bad boy. I'm going to get in trouble for saying this, but women are sometimes attracted to rogues and sometimes even marry them. So there is this iron wall between this likable bad boy and his wife who is running for president. She can say, "I don't know anything about Dubai; I can't be responsible for their policies; it's not my problem." She can get away with that because the media has cut her a lot of slack, so far.
>
> The decision was made in the Clinton camp that theirs would not be a passive relationship, that she would say, "Hey, if you elect me,

you're going to get him in the office." So there's duplicity at work here. On the one hand, she bears no responsibility for anything negative about him. But if she's elected, he's going to be in the White House with his charm and his experience and his wisdom. So she's trying to have it both ways. Can that work? We'll see.

If Hillary Clinton is elected president, there will be a relationship with her spouse that is unprecedented in American history. First ladies in the past were essentially extensions of their husbands. The most political first ladies were Eleanor Roosevelt, who had a political agenda of her own which was different than her husband's. And of course First Lady Hillary Clinton was given assignments. But now we could have a "first man" in the White House who is a lobbyist, who has business dealings. This is new territory for the American story.

For another viewpoint on Bill Clinton's relationship with Dubai, we turn again to best-selling author and terrorism analyst Richard Miniter:

What's more interesting about this, as it relates to a Hillary Clinton presidency, is the behavior of the fellow who would be first man.

From the moment he left the White House until January 2007, Bill Clinton earned in excess of $62 million. That's an extraordinary amount of money for anyone to earn over a lifetime, let alone over six years. Unlike other ex-presidents, Clinton is not specializing in charity. He has made money, $62 million, and what does he owe in return?

Some of his benefactors have agendas quite different from the interests of the United States. As a private citizen, if he wants to take the money, fine—it's a free country. But will Hillary Clinton as president have to serve the interests of a company that paid her husband so many millions of dollars? That's a legitimate question.

Do we really want to elect someone whose husband is financially entwined with some very foreign and very secretive corporations?

Reporter Amanda Carpenter also spoke to the larger implications of Bill Clinton out there working as a highly paid lobbyist:

As a former president, he's entitled to make money—the more the merrier, I say. It's how he makes his money that matters, right?

When Ronald Reagan made money after his presidency, the *New York Times* ran an editorial accusing him of selling the presidency—all for the $2.5 million he was paid. Now we don't hear much from the *New York Times* when Bill Clinton earns more than $60 million, most of it from foreign governments.

He goes to the United Emirates to make money. He goes to Colombia to make money. He speaks to people opposed to a free Taiwan. He criticizes the sitting president in overseas venues—which is something past presidents refrained from doing.

He is highly paid to promote green energy while Senator Clinton is pushing for federal subsidies for green energy. She has routed federal money to companies that produce green energy. She has also been trying to enact legislation for a "strategic energy fund" that would tax oil companies, put those tax dollars into a fund, then let government divvy it up to companies producing green energy, hybrids, ethanol. Okay. But which green companies would get these taxpayer funds?

The companies Bill Clinton is working for! Any conflicts of interest here? Any ethical lapses?

So what kind of impact would the first man have on a Hillary presidency? Author and Washington editor of the *National Review* Kate O'Beirne offers a riposte:

Just as Hillary Clinton told the American public in 1992 that if they vote for Bill Clinton, they get the two of them—like a blue-plate special—already she is telling the public that if they vote for her in

2008, they will also get Bill Clinton. It should give voters reason to pause when they contemplate Bill Clinton back in the White House, with time on his hands. Would we have the commander in chief sleeping with the lobbyist in chief, though who knows who the lobbyist in chief would be sleeping with?

SHADES OF "I VOTED FOR THE WAR
BEFORE I VOTED AGAINST IT"

Friends of Hillary say she has tried very hard to avoid the Kerry '04 trap of being captured on national television saying that he voted *for* war funding before he voted *against* it. That single statement launched a thousand Republican attacks and, perhaps more than anything else, cost John Kerry the election.

But wanting to avoid an embarrassing obvious flip-flop and succeeding at it are very two different kettles of fish, given the political landscape that Hillary must operate in. All of the participants in our film and quoted in this book had strong opinions and insights into the current war in Iraq. To set the stage, we'll first review the major statements that Hillary has made on the war on Iraq, with commentary from national security expert Michael Ledeen, Freedom Scholar at the American Enterprise Institute:

CITIZENS UNITED: In 1998, Hillary said, "Saddam Hussein has used these chemical weapons against his own people . . . action against Saddam Hussein is in the long-term interest of our national security."

LEDEEN: It was certainly true that Saddam Hussein had used chemical weapons against his own people, and against Iranians, without the slightest remorse. So it was reasonable to conclude that he would be willing to do it again. The removal of Saddam Hussein was in the best long-term interest of American national security.

CITIZENS UNITED: Then in 2002, Hillary said, "Facts on Saddam's weapons of mass destruction are not in doubt. . . . Saddam obstructed the weapons inspectors work. . . . Saddam has given aid to al-Qaeda . . . the authority to use force is inherent in the original 1991 United Nations Resolution, as President Clinton recognized, when he launched Operation Desert Fox in 1998."

LEDEEN: Clearly at this time Hillary is firmly committed in her support of the war, as evidenced by a statement a year later, in 2003, that the war should last however long it takes, and that patience is required. She was right about that. Patience is very important in war. I mean, the Cold War lasted fifty years. Often over those fifty years, people came along and said, "Enough already." You can find a lot of statements on the floor of the Senate, made by a lot of famous senators, asking why we still have troops in South Korea, why we still have troops in Germany, why we installed the Ural missiles in the 1980s to respond to the Soviet offensive, why, why, why? So when Hillary argued for staying the course, that was the right position.

CITIZENS UNITED: Two more years pass, and Hillary was rejecting calls for a rigid timetable for withdrawal from Iraq. She said she was not comfortable setting exit strategies. She said, "Immediate withdrawal would be a big mistake."

LEDEEN: Right on every count. And importantly, it's not up to a legislator to try to outguess the military strategists. That's not their job. If a legislator does not like the war, then cut off the money. They're entitled to do that. But once you start down the path of having five or six hundred secretaries of defense, it's obviously hopeless. No good can come of that.

CITIZENS UNITED: And that brings us to June 2007 and suddenly Hillary said, "The troops should come home . . . this is George Bush's war."

LEDEEN: And she has moved to de-authorize the war and repudiate her earlier votes. So that would represent a complete turnabout. She is now talking about withdrawal and about setting a firm date for withdrawal.

CITIZENS UNITED: If I'm a world leader, and Hillary Clinton wins, what kind of foreign policy can I expect from her?

LEDEEN: Never mind if I'm a world leader, which presents a whole larger set of problems. What if I'm Prime Minister al-Maliki of Iraq? I know I've got Bush to contend with now. But I read the *New York Times* every day. I watch the evening news, or my people do and tell me what's on it. I talk to Democrats. They come and talk to me, and they tell me that they're going to keep voting against this war, and they're going to clear out of Iraq when they win the White House. So what will I, al-Maliki, do under those circumstances?

I'm going to start abusing my enemies! Because the Americans are going to be gone, and the Syrians and Iranians are still going to be there, right next door. I can't defend myself against Syria and Iran—I know that.

You see, al-Maliki came to power from an underground Shiite organization run by Iranians. He knows how lethal they are. If he's not confident in American protection, he's going to run. Everybody's going to run.

Michael Medved looks at Hillary's evolving positions on the Iraq War and wonders if she has the courage required of a commander in chief:

One of my favorite childhood books was *Profiles in Courage* by John F. Kennedy. Actually, Theodore Sorensen wrote it, but Kennedy took credit. This book told of people who fought against incredible odds to tell the truth, people who did the right thing rather than pander to the whims and caprice of the moment. I admire that kind of political courage.

Joe Lieberman is an example of it.

John McCain is an example of it.

Hillary Clinton is not an example, and it's a shame.

She could have been a very plausible presidential candidate for moderate voters and independent voters by sticking with her positions on Iraq. But she's trying to have it every which way . . . and loose.

On the one hand, she tells the *New York Times* in a March 14, 2007, interview that there should be a "significant military force there to fight al-Qaeda, deter Iranian aggression, protect the Kurds and possibly support the Iraqi military." That's honest; that's real. And she says it in unequivocal terms. She sounds like McCain, or Bush for that matter. And good for her!

Then out on the campaign stump she says, "The first thing I will do when I am elected your president is bring our troops home." And she gets big applause from left-wing partisans. Okay, but which is it? You, you can't have it both ways.

One Hillary says she's going to bring the troops home right away; the other Hillary says she's going to keep troops in Iraq indefinitely.

One of these two women is lying.

Political commentator Bay Buchanan wonders whether Hillary is taking the political expedient road or if she's just lost:

Some people say, "She's flipping; she's flopping." No, she's lying. She's refusing to take responsibility for asking our brave soldiers to put their lives on the line. You cannot have a commander in chief who will not stand behind the troops.

How could Hillary vote to send our own forces overseas—to ask our brave young men and women to sacrifice their lives, and then, when the war became politically unpopular, vote to withdraw her support for the troops?

She says that the only reason she voted for the war resolution was because the president lied to her. She says she did not know it was for war. Well, how can she ask us to make her president when she can't even understand the wording of a war resolution?

But let's go a step further: how could she not have understood the war resolution when she defended the war for two years before she opposed the war? This makes no sense.

Larry Kudlow, host of CNBC's *Kudlow & Company*, says that Hillary's personality is dependent on the personality of her Democratic Party:

Mrs. Clinton has had so many different positions on Iraq that right away there's a problem. If the Iraq story does improve, that's going to be very hard for Democrats. They're heavily invested in Iraq War failure. Mrs. Clinton is now invested in Iraq War failure. Some of that is to appease the nutcases in the left wing of her party. Some of it she may believe.

The bigger issue here, as I see it, is whether the Democrats are going to continue to go down the McGovern path—weak on national security. The grass roots of the party are hard lefties. Now in the old days the candidate would capture the grass roots and then move to the center of the political spectrum. That is not so easy anymore. We have 24/7 video, and folks can instantly capture and repeat whatever is said. Mrs. Clinton is going to have a problem with that.

It's an odd story because Mrs. Clinton did work hard as a rookie member of the Armed Services Committee. She was quite reasonable in supporting President Bush initially on the war in Iraq. Her husband, of course, was the first person to call for a regime change in Iraq, and that was in 1998. She will have to live that down. It's going to be hard for her to wriggle out of these past positions.

Jeff Gerth, author and Pulitzer Prize winner, offers a window into the backroom arm-twisting Hillary pulled off to try to look credible as she flip-flopped on the war:

In the June 2007 debate in New Hampshire, when Hillary was trying to come across as more dovish, she insisted that she had long favored using diplomacy to deal with Iraq. Yet if you look at her record on the floor of the Senate in October of 2002, you see that she supported the war authorization bill, which *did not* have any requirement of diplomacy. Now—and this is important—just hours before that vote, there was an amendment called the Levin Amendment, which required the U.S. to use diplomacy. Hillary voted against the Levin Amendment. Not only did she vote against it, she didn't even bother to go to the Senate floor to participate while for ninety-five minutes that amendment was debated. So Hillary was bound to be caught.

Then in another speech Hillary said she had supported the Byrd Amendment of 2002 because it allowed the president to go to war only for one year. She was trying to portray herself as being "only half for the war, maybe against the war, before I actually voted for it." Now as it turns out, she was mistaken. The Byrd Amendment actually said that the president had to come back to Congress every twelve months and say whether or not he wanted to continue pursuing the war. Everybody in Congress knew that was a meaningless amendment, because it amounted to nothing more than a regular briefing from the president. But in her speech, Hillary was hoping to distort her position and pretend she was sort of *against* the war before she voted for the war. Essentially, she stepped into a quagmire.

Hillary was trying to avoid the John Kerry flip-flop by not apologizing for her vote. But she's created a different set of flip-flops by her own distortion of the record and her attempt to portray herself as being for diplomacy and being sort of against the war when, in fact, her record is quite the opposite. And it slapped her hard! In June 2006, she appeared at a conference of a liberal antiwar group. She got up and said we should not put a timetable on withdrawal from Iraq. She got booed!

So what did she do after getting booed? The very next day she showed up at a private meeting of about a dozen senators who had been meeting about Iraq. Hillary had never been to one of these meetings before. But she showed up, muscled her way into the debate, and started projecting herself as a leader on this issue.

The group's leader, Harry Reid, was trying to get agreement on an amendment that could be introduced on the floor of Congress. He asked Senator Feinstein to sponsor it, because he didn't want any presidential aspirants sponsoring it, mucking it up politically. Senator Feinstein said fine.

A couple days later, the amendment rolled out. And on that day Hillary intervened with Harry Reid and got herself named as a co-sponsor. It was actually *handwritten* into the legislation!

Of course Hillary's purpose in doing this was to burnish her credentials as someone working to phase out American involvement in Iraq, someone who's a leader in the Senate on national security affairs. Sure enough, when she announced her run for president and set up her Web site, she touted her role as a leader on national security.

The bottom line: Hillary had been against the war before she was for it, before she was against it all over again.

Washington reporter Amanda Carpenter tried to interview Hillary while Hillary's wartime positions were evolving:

> Now Hillary never speaks openly to the media, but I caught her in the railway beneath the Senate building, and I asked her, "So, do you think George Tenet falsified that information in the intelligence report? Because the only way Bush could have lied to get us into war was if George Tenet lied to him."
>
> Of course Hillary's smart, and she knows where I'm headed with this question, and she gives me a quintessential Clinton answer. She says, "That's one of those important matters the intelligence committee needs to look into."
>
> So I followed up right way with, "Did you read the National Intelligence Estimate, which outlined the case for war? George Tenet compiled it. It represented the very best intelligence we had at the time." And she says, "The intelligence committee really needs to look into that." And funny how things turn out. . . .
>
> A couple months ago, a reporter yelled out to her, "Senator Clinton, did you read the National Intelligence Estimate?" And she replied, "No. I was briefed." She didn't read it! Only senators are allowed into a special room to read these briefings—it's all very secure. Staff aides are not allowed in to read on behalf of their senators. So most likely, she was lying and wasn't even briefed on the contents of the intelligence report. Not impressive for someone aspiring to be president.

Tony Blankley, former editor of the editorial page of the *Washington Times*, speaks to the problems Hillary will have with voters if Iraq turns out to be a success as the 2008 elections near:

> If Iraq proves to be a success in the public's mind by November 2008, then Hillary will look to have been unnecessarily defeatist and will

probably lose the election. She's going to try to maneuver as much as she can, but she is now deeply invested in defeat.

I don't think she wanted to be defeatist on the war. But she found herself pulled there, and was willing to go there to harvest those left-wing votes in the primary.

Newt Gingrich sums up Hillary's wild ride in her pursuit of the presidency:

I feel almost embarrassed for her. She's being pushed to the left by the activist antiwar militant Democrats. Watch her gradually, slowly, inch-by-inch, and you can almost track this evolution away from what I think she really believes, toward what she thinks she has to say to get the nomination. I think that it's a bit sad. But on the other hand, "profiles in courage" aren't all that common in candidates for the presidency.

HILLARY SAYS SHE SUPPORTS THE TROOPS—DO THEY AGREE?

Amanda Carpenter's brother is a United States Marine:

I know from talking to my brother and his friends that nothing scares them more than Hillary Clinton as commander in chief. And it's not because she is a woman; it's because she cannot be trusted.

Guys in the military are tough. They don't want to badmouth politicians. But when you have a politician who has no military experience, who has a past of showing disrespect for the military, who clearly does not understand how the military in the field do their job, and who now says she wants to cut funding for operations in Iraq, well, that just totally invalidates their mission, and you won't find many friends among them.

DOES HILLARY'S VOTING RECORD
EMBOLDEN OUR ENEMIES?

When Hillary votes to deauthorize funding for our troops in Iraq, it sends one message to our soldiers, another to our allies, and still another to our enemies. Richard Miniter reports on the conversation he had at a dinner party in Baghdad recently:

> I was dining with a member of the Iraqi Parliament, a Sunni Muslim. And he said, "I wish your media and politicians would stop talking about a withdrawal. It just makes all of the people who were pro-American in the Iraqi government want to cut side-deals with the Iranians, because if the Americans are going to leave soon, the Iranians are going to be the victors."
>
> My friend also said, "When your media portrays the insurgents as doing well against the Americans, the people on Baghdad's streets think the insurgents must be doing really, really well against the Americans." People on the streets just assume the U.S. media would be trying to make the Americans look good. They are not versed in the ways of a free press; they grew up in Arab lands with a strictly controlled press.
>
> The truth of Iraq, as clearly evidenced by those of us who regularly visit Iraq, is that the insurgents are outnumbered, they're outgunned, and they're increasingly being defeated.
>
> Now in the beginning of the Iraq War, it looked like Senator Clinton was going to be tough. She not only voted for the Iraq War, but she argued for it in the well of the U.S. Senate. One of the points she made repeatedly was that if we fail to attack our enemies decisively, we will embolden them. She said that if we talk a tough game but don't appear to back it up, then we make ourselves hollow and open to attack.

Flash forward three years, and she claims to be outraged when a senior Pentagon official tells her the very same thing—that all her new talk of withdrawal is simply encouraging our enemies.

This experience of watching Hillary shift her position on Iraq tells us principally that she is not a leader but a follower. The question for voters in this election is: Who is Hillary following now, and whoever that is, do they have the best interests of the United States in mind?

Clare Lopez, strategic policy and intelligence expert, reports on how our enemies turn Hillary's statements into tools to kill our troops in the field:

When Senator Clinton and others in the Democratic leadership talk about defunding the effort in Iraq, about withdrawing from the war on terror, the American people are not the only ones listening. Our enemies are listening as well. They hear the calls to pack up and go home. They know that the will of the American people can be sapped from the inside. They know our national psyche, they know our weaknesses . . . and they see it expressed in people such as Hillary Clinton.

They have worked hard to abet this weakness on our homefront and are now working just as hard to turn our weakness into their strength in recruiting. They're telling men to join the jihad and beat America!

All the enemy has to do is show their recruits video of Hillary on the campaign trail.

What's more, as they see mounting evidence that the U.S. has lost the will to fight in Iraq—the central battlefield in this war—then they will be emboldened to fight in other places. Iraq is not a self-contained discrete battlefield. It is an important battlefield, but it's not the only one. And if we cede that geography to the enemy, they will use it as a launching pad to expand elsewhere.

Frank Gaffney believes that our enemies are watching this election closely to gain clues about the next steps to take:

If I were a bad guy looking at the United States today, I'd be cheering for Hillary Clinton to be president of the United States. I don't know that they are, but it stands to reason given what they've seen of her.

| 5 |

HOW MUCH WOULD HILLARYCARE COST US *THIS* TIME?

Hillary's first attempt in 1993–94 to prove her political skills on the national stage was widely viewed as one of the most embarrassing legislative disasters in our nation's history. In trying to overhaul the entire U.S. healthcare system all at once, Hillary set a great many "needed" reforms back decades. The bill was a complex proposal running more than one thousand pages and criticized as being overly bureaucratic and restrictive of patient choice. U.S. senator Daniel Patrick Moynihan indicated "anyone who thinks [the Clinton healthcare plan] can work in the real world as presently written isn't living in it."

Now Hillary has unveiled the outlines of HillaryCare II, hoping to get it right the second time. We spoke with two practicing physicians and a number of healthcare reporters and authorities to find out the costs we could expect on a second go-round.

WHERE SOCIALIZED MEDICINE
ALREADY EXISTS, WHAT'S THE COST?

Dr. Lee Hieb is an orthopedic spine surgeon with several decades of medical experience. Now practicing in Yuma, Arizona, she offers a frontline view of medicine the way Hillary likes it:

> Almost 70 percent of my patients are on Medicare, 25 percent on a state-run medical program called Access, and 2 percent [on] private insurance. Yuma is already operating under a very socialized medical environment.
>
> We deal with the federal and state government all the time. And as the third fastest growing community in America, we have a serious shortage of physicians. We also have a large number of uninsured patients. I think our number is higher than most places because we have a lot of people crossing the border who do not have insurance—some illegals, but mostly legals. Whether legal or not, many of these uninsured have made an economic decision about healthcare.
>
> They've determined that they can spend their money on other things—cars, motorcycles, toys—and not worry about buying insurance because they know we'll take care of them anyway. They know that when they come to the emergency room, they're not going to be denied care.
>
> When medical care is given away, it is not valued. It's always easier to spend somebody else's money. For example:
>
> A woman came to the emergency room with a sprained foot. I was on call, and I attended to her foot. In talking with her, I learned that earlier that day she had walked into the emergency room—the sprain was a minor one, obviously—but the waiting list was six hours long. So she drove herself home and called an ambulance. The ambulance brought her in, and she went to the head of the line!

As I opened her chart, I discovered that the state—that is, the taxpayers—had paid for her ambulance ride.

In the old days, before you or I would spend our own money on a minor medical problem, we would go to a friend or parent and say, "What do you think I should do about this problem?" Whether it was your kid's sniffily nose or your sprained foot, you would try to take care of it yourself. Now it's easy to just go to the emergency room—because you're not paying for it, not paying directly anyway. That's a big problem when we give free medical care to people.

Dr. Mitch Freeman is another veteran physician who also works shifts in the emergency room in Yuma Regional Medical Center. He sees a lot of patients who have free medical access:

The sad truth is—when you give something to people for free, they abuse it and overuse it, because there's no accountability.

I saw a five-year-old child one day in the emergency room; she was there because she had a "pink eye" the day before. The day I saw her, she was fine. When people are made accountable for their medical decisions, they don't abuse the medical system or overload the emergency room or come in for pink eye that's healed!

If you go to the labor and delivery floor in Yuma Regional, about 80 percent of the women are low income. They're having everything done for free and not paying one penny. But if you're working for a living and you're paying for insurance, you have a big premium and out-of-pocket expenses for these pregnancy and delivery services.

Hillary maintains that we are a big, prosperous, compassionate nation, and if there are people among us who cannot afford to pay for healthcare, then we owe it to ourselves to help them. To which Dr. Lee Hieb responds:

I don't think I'd be a physician if I didn't care about helping people. My dad was a physician; my son wants to be a physician—we love what we do; we love helping people. But having real, genuine compassion for people means making things better for people.

When we talk about making things better through affordable healthcare, what does that mean?

Does it mean we give people Cadillac care? Hyundai care? Certainly there's a basic level of care that everybody should be able to buy into. But the government has made medical care so expensive that even hardworking people can't afford their health insurance premiums.

Now I'll be the first to admit that our American system is not perfect. And some folks will fall through the cracks in any system you have. But the great history of government-run systems, to my understanding, is a history of increasing costs and decreasing quality.

The liberal mantra is: let's have the type of care that England and France and Canada have! But a lot of people don't realize the poor quality of care those people are experiencing.

The breast cancer death rate is higher in England and Canada than it is in the United States. Why is that? Because in England and Canada you have to wait an average of two months after your biopsy to get treatment—that can lead to serious problems.

One of our doctors here had a patient from England who asked, "Please, take out my gall bladder before I go back to England." She had been on a waiting list for four years to get her gall bladder removed in England. Here in the states, she got it removed right away. Unfortunately, it turned out that she had a cancerous gall bladder, and she died. It was very sad. But if she had been an American citizen, she wouldn't have died—because she would not have waited four years!

Medical care is free in Mexico. It's free in Canada. It's free in the Soviet Union. But people cross the border all the time or fly in on

Aeroflot to get their care in the U.S. because they simply can't get what they want from the socialized medicine they have in their countries.

Hillary takes the opposing view. She maintains that every industrialized nation has more government-provided healthcare than the United States and that we are creating an economic burden by not having more.

HILLARY CLAIMS HER HEALTHCARE PLAN WILL SAVE MONEY

Larry Kudlow, who worked in the Office of Management and Budget under President Reagan, explains why U.S. medical insurance costs so much:

> One of the main reasons insurance is so expensive is that government policies prevent competition among insurance companies. That will be a key issue in this election. There needs to be interstate competition so that people in New York, for instance, can shop in Illinois if they want for a policy that suits them. They can shop for Cadillac coverage or Chevy coverage—whatever their wallet can tolerate. This is the surest way to bring insurance costs down. Government rules and regulations have shut down any real competition in healthcare, and as a result, the costs have skyrocketed. Competition will bring down costs.
>
> Mrs. Clinton doesn't seem to like the rough-and-tumble of the marketplace. When the oil companies were making money, for example, she said we should take their profits and put them into a government fund to create alternative energy. Well, that's a nice socialist vision, circa Soviet Union 1975. But in America we have a tradition called constitutional liberty.
>
> Here in America, if you incorporate and make money, you pay

your taxes, and it's your money after that. The Exxons of the world have paid a fortune in taxes—they should be Hillary's best friends. But she wants to take more from them. This is one of her weakest traits. It's the Al Gore disease. In 2000, Al Gore ran for president, oddly enough, not on his record of economic success, but against corporations. He decided to be a business basher, a real populist. And you know what? He lost a race he should have won by ten percentage points.

If Mrs. Clinton goes down that route, she'll get clobbered. Two out of every three voters own shares of stock in U.S. corporations. I haven't heard a single Democrat, with the possible exception of [New Mexico governor] Bill Richardson, even acknowledge the investor class. But how many shareholders does Exxon have? Millions! It has been one of the greatest corporations in the history of America—throwing off returns for firemen, for police, for teachers. Now Hillary wants to penalize Exxon and, in so doing, penalize millions of Americans?

Apparently Hillary not only wants to further tax corporations, she also wants to tax the rich to pay for healthcare. That's what she has been telling middle-class Americans who can't afford their insurance premiums. The economists we interviewed for our film had plenty to say about this, starting with Dick Armey:

The real rate of taxes is the level of government spending. So we're all going to pay for it, and Hillary is just demagoguing. But what's the real cost of a national healthcare system?

When every physician in America becomes an employee of the state, and has their right to practice medicine prescribed to them by a bunch of bureaucrats who have never even had an anatomy course, probably a bunch of undergraduate sociology majors fresh out of school, the willingness to practice medicine is going to go down. The willingness to suffer through eight years of medical school is going to go down.

We'll have a shortage of good doctors because the good ones will have gone elsewhere.

We will have the problems they have in Canada. Everything Hillary wants for America is what Canada does for its people, any one of whom with five extra bucks in their pocket comes across the border to the United States for healthcare services. I have a friend from Canada who says, "Don't you Americans do what we've done; if you do, we Canadians will have no place to go."

If America gives up this freedom to choose, if we bleed away the vitality of a market based healthcare system, where do folks go for the best care? There has to be a place where people can go for the best. If it's not going to be America, where's it going to be?

They might go to Europe, ironically, suggests economist Larry Kudlow:

Hillary worships the old Europe model—the big government social democracy model. But interestingly, Europe has been moving away from that model. France, for example, is trying to offer more choice in healthcare. There has been a clamoring for private hospitals, doctors, and clinics because government-run programs don't work; the lines are too long; you can't get the drugs you need.

Nicolas Sarcozi, the new president of France, is trying to move France into the twenty-first century with tax cuts, more competition, and less government. So it would be a pity if Senator Clinton decided we want to be France in the '80s and '90s when France wants to be the United States in the twenty-first century.

If we set about raising taxes and expanding the public sector, we might see the time when France passes us by. I hope that's never true, but we might see that time.

Let's assume Hillary wins and "affordable healthcare for everyone" becomes more than a slogan; it becomes policy. How would it be executed? Dr. Lee Hieb, a board certified orthopedic surgeon specializing in spinal surgery, has some questions and answers:

If healthcare were free to all, what would be covered? Would everyone have access to free ambulance rides? Free aromatherapy treatments? Free nose jobs? Free breast implants? Or would we simply commit to caring for people we find bleeding on the street? There are a lot of gray areas. I think we would all agree that we don't want to leave people lying in the street. But who makes these decisions? Some bureaucrat in Washington?

At present, we have a situation where the uninsured get pretty much the same treatment as someone paying full boat for insurance. We allow those who don't pay a dime to enjoy the finest in medical care, along with private hospital rooms, a color TV, and all the amenities. Is this the way it should be?

In the old days, through the charity hospitals, we took care of everyone who needed help—we just gave them care in a less expensive fashion. It made sense—economically and morally. But then government stepped in with all their mandates and requirements, and they drove up the cost.

Take the cost of a CAT scan. If I order a scan of an entire body in the Medicare facility here, it costs $24,000—plus the cost of a doctor's interpretation. But if I travel up to Phoenix and am willing to pay cash, it costs $1,000—and that includes a visit with the doctor. They take cash, they take credit cards, but they don't take insurance or Medicare.

ARE DOCTORS THE BIGGEST VICTIMS
IN THE HEALTHCARE DEBATE?

In an open market, there are *many* incentives to drive down prices and continually improve service. In a government-run system, there are *few* incentives to lower prices or improve quality, says Dr. Lee Hieb:

Government is always good in little doses. We have building codes so that people don't build fire traps—to a certain degree, that makes sense. On the other hand, those building codes have caused me to spend thousands of dollars unnecessarily on my office—just because some bureaucrat wanted to get his imprint on the code. It's the same with medicine. The first set of standards we received from the government were worthwhile—they made things better. But now it's out of control, adding untold cost and frustration to medicine.

For every two nurses you have at your bedside, for example, you need another nurse out in the pen doing paperwork. Fifty percent more nurses to see patients now because of Medicare regulations.

There are over one hundred thousand pages of regulations, and doctors can't hope to understand them all, much less follow them! It's a very inefficient engine. And Hillary wants to give us more?

I don't exaggerate when I say that government actively sabotages quality medicine by forcing too much time with paperwork and too little time with patients.

I mean, what is the major complaint people have with doctors? People feel they don't get enough time with their doctor, or worse yet, they don't have access to their doctor. With the plans we see coming from Hillary, it's going to get worse.

Orthopedic surgeons require four years of college, four years of medical school, five years of residency, and often another two years in a specialty fellowship and even a year of research. That's a lot of years, and it begins with a med school debt of $200,000. How many people are going to put themselves through all this—only to come into a system where your income is restricted, your every move is proscribed by some bureaucrat in Washington, and your patients increasingly come to despise you because you're the human face of a system that doesn't work?

I feel depressed about what's happening, because I think this great medical debate will go one of two ways: I would hope that we wake up and realize we don't want the medical system that Canada or England has; we want one-on-one doctor-patient interaction. But what I'm afraid is going to happen is that government will tell doctors like me, "We are no longer going to grant you a medical license unless you participate in government-run medicine." And that will be the death knell of medicine.

Dr. Mitch Freeman became so thoroughly disgusted with the red tape and hassles of Medicare, he stopped accepting it. Doctors across America may find that his experiences resonate with their own:

I opted completely out of Medicare because they make it harder to conduct business and help people.

Maybe the government will come up with some wonderful solution to the healthcare mess, but so far every medical system from the government has created more problems and more red tape.

The worst part of Medicare is the billing—they make it hard to bill correctly. And if you are a doctor and you have a question that needs answering, forget about getting any "customer service" out of the government. If you call ten times and ask the same question, you get ten answers, and none of them will be right. They don't have to be accountable, but you do, or there's hell to pay.

If you get audited by Medicare, they can pull ten patient billing records. If two of those records billed high, and three of the records billed low, you would think the government would be happy—might even be willing to reimburse for underbilling. But no. They would say, "You overbilled! We'll multiply the overbillings we discovered by the number of patient visits you had, and that will be the fine we'll assess you. If you don't pay it, we can put you in jail and take your license. We can screw you up basically."

In her defense of government-run healthcare, Hillary claims she can drive efficiencies that that will save the nation $120 billion and save individuals $2,200 a year. That sounds like a good deal, right? Former House majority leader Dick Armey looks at Hillary's numbers:

Hillary throws around a lot of numbers on the campaign trail. But it doesn't pass the BS meter. Politicians promise, but when do they deliver? Where have you seen the government make anything more efficient and less costly by its presence? Look at the postal service—you want those people running healthcare?

What motivation will they have to provide a quality service? If you're in the private sector, you want to perform well because that will attract customers. If you're in government, you've got a mandate. Folks have to come to you—they have no choice—so you have no incentive to be good.

Border towns like Yuma pose unique challenges for medical professionals, but the stories Dr. Lee Hieb tells could be told in any number of towns across America:

One patient of mine was actually a drug runner who had for years used his green card to cross the border to buy and sell drugs. Well, apparently he messed up with Mr. Big, and to teach him a lesson, they blew a hole in his foot with a shotgun down in Mexico. He went to a hospital, but even he recognized that free care is not always good care—they were going to amputate his foot. So he hopped up to the border, literally hopped, and at that point demanded an ambulance. By law, we had to comply.

Preparing for surgery, I learned that this outlaw had Medicare. He was a healthy twenty-five-year-old guy on Medicare!

Turns out he had been involved in a gangland shooting in the States and his head was grazed by a bullet; he was told he had a seizure disorder—not that we ever saw this when he was in our care—and from that day forward he received total Social Security disability.

When I saw him, he was chained to the bed and there was a federal marshal at his side. Turns out, he was also wanted on four federal warrants. So I asked the marshal, "This guy has been wanted for years on four federal warrants, but we're giving him his Social Security check every two weeks?"

The marshal explained that by an act of Congress, you can't trace people using their Social Security check. I was appalled, and it must have been obvious. He looked at me like I had just fallen off the turnip truck. "That's how they afford their drug running," he said, "because their groceries and such can be paid for with the Social Security check."

Government has created this perverse system that rewards people who really shouldn't be in the system at all, at the expense of other people who should be. Now imagine this government system expanding across the whole trillion dollar realm of healthcare!

One of the more shocking moments in our interviews came when Dr. Lee Hieb spoke of the potential dangers of government-run healthcare:

With the new electronic billing and medical record mandates from the government, we're getting to the point where a government bureaucrat can push a button and review the psychiatric history of anybody he wants to. I think that's a dangerous precedent.

I don't think it's a good idea to have everybody's health information digitized in a way that people who don't really care about you have access to it. But that's where we're headed, bit by bit.

Consider this: the first German socialized medicine program was set up by the kaiser to keep control of the population. If you make people beholden to you for their very health, you've got them by the throat. What happened to the detailed personal records that the Germans kept on their citizens? Well, the Nazis made efficient use of them in their euthanasia program.

When in 1993 Hillary launched her first assault on healthcare, she took her plan up to Capitol Hill and appeared before the Education Committee, where she was confronted by Congressman Dick Armey:

> It was a bit of a stunner for us. Of course, we'd watched the campaign and we could see that as Clinton said: we were going to get two for the price of one. But for our president to say, "I have put the first lady in charge of one of the biggest policy initiatives in the last fifteen to twenty years," it was amazing!
>
> Next we learned that she had lots of resources at her disposal. You don't bring in Ira Magaziner and his crowd for nothing. Ira Magaziner is a left-wing architect who specialized in building complex systems that don't work. And so Hillary brought him in, and they spent a lot of money in secret, not telling anybody what they were doing.

Another firsthand witness to HillaryCare I was Newt Gingrich:

Certainly you have to ask whether or not she learned anything from that experience. It was a failure. She knows it was a failure—a very embarrassing failure for her. She tried to do far too much, and her leftist allies wouldn't allow her to compromise at all. So the health-care reform she could have achieved was lost—her supporters would not tolerate anything except absolute victory on their terms.

I think the combination of the big tax increase of 1993, the left-wing social policies, the effort to take guns from Americans, and the healthcare debacle all made possible the Contract with America and the election of the first House majority for Republicans in forty years.

Participants in our film were divided on whether Hillary Clinton learned anything from her healthcare battles in the early 1990s. But there was consensus on which way she'll lean should she be formulating new healthcare policy.

Townhall.com reporter Amanda Carpenter put it the most simply:

Hillary says she can be trusted to bring up healthcare again because she had the scars to show for it. Well, the scars don't mean her health-care plan is pretty. She is still an advocate for universal healthcare. The fact that she flubbed it the first time is no reason to let her do it again.

Author and FOX News correspondent Angela McGlowan has watched Hillary's evolving positions on healthcare and admits to not knowing what to expect:

In 1992, Hillary stood for socialized medicine. But in 2006, only one senator took *more* campaign donations from pharmaceutical companies, drug companies, and healthcare companies than Hillary took.

So is she for socialized medicine? Is she for publicly traded healthcare companies? I don't know. With Hillary Clinton, you only know that she'll be standing whichever way the wind is blowing.

Former congressman Dick Armey expects the same ole, same ole healthcare:

Hillary has not given up on a bad idea. And once she gets her mind set on something, she gets what we from Texas call a case of the "bound to"—she's going to do it if she gets the authority to do it.

And with the Republicans performing poorly these days, Hillary could win the White House and have a Democrat-controlled House and Senate. That means we'll get a national healthcare plan without any real debate. And "business" will buy into her plan. Why?

Lots of businesses are reeling under the burden of their healthcare legacy costs; they would be happy to support a plan that lets them dump their obligations off on the government (which means us taxpayers).

A handy ending to this healthcare discussion comes from Hillary's closest advisor, Bill Clinton. In his new book *Giving: How Each of Us Can Change the World* (Knopf, 2007), he wrote that Hillary's healthcare plan was victimized by politics, not that it was bad policy.

We have two responses—the first from Tony Blankley:

This is typical Clintonian spin. Almost every faction in American political society attacked her proposal because it was bad policy for almost every faction of American healthcare. It was bad politics because it was bad policy. And, of course, Hillary understands that. She has subsequently backed off and said her healthcare plan was a mistake. So in writing his book, I suppose Bill forgot to get the story straight with his own wife.

And second from Larry Kudlow:

The effort to kill HillaryCare was good common sense. Americans know a bad fish when they smell one. The Clintons misjudged the smarts of the American voter on that one. There is no reason to tear down our system of free enterprise—whether for healthcare or anything else. That was the biggest mistake they made. If they go down that road again, they will suffer the same huge political loss they suffered in the 1990s. Let's hope we don't see that terrible waste all over again.

6

ASSESSING HILLARY'S PERFORMANCE AS A SENATOR

In 1992, Bill Clinton said that with his candidacy, voters could "buy one, get one free," meaning that if you voted for him, you also got Hillary Clinton as part of the deal.

The participants in our film and quoted in this book cited examples of the Clintons working as a team, and also quite the opposite. But almost everyone agreed that when Hillary made a run for the Senate seat in New York, she was running on her own merits. Sure, she was carpetbagging. Sure, she was trading on her husband's famous name. But those were avenues and assets available to her, so why not use them? Bottom line, she was her own woman.

So once in office as a senator, how did Hillary perform? It's fair to say that her record as a senator offers the closest analogy to the type of accomplishments we might expect of her presidency.

SENATOR CLINTON'S VOTING RECORD

We asked political consultant Dick Morris to look at Senator Clinton's record:

In two terms in the Senate, Hillary has authored about twenty pieces of legislation. Let me tell you what some of them were:

To commemorate the 225th anniversary of the American Revolution.

To express our appreciation to Alexander Hamilton.

To name the Thurgood Marshall courthouse in lower Manhattan.

To honor the men's and the women's lacrosse teams from Syracuse High School.

To express the sense of Congress that Harriet Tubman, who died over a hundred years ago, should have received a federal pension.

To name a post office after a firefighter who died on 9/11.

Of substantive pieces of legislation, she's passed only five. Three of them relate to 9/11—they were passed unanimously, and the whole New York delegation sponsored them. There are only two important bills to credit to Hillary. One was a very good bill increasing nurses' salaries and recruitment. The second one provided respite care for people dealing with Alzheimer's patients. Good bills. But is it gravitas enough to elect a president of the United States?

Hillary did manage to route federal money back to New York. Amanda Carpenter offers a couple examples of the bacon Clinton brought home:

In the weeks after 9/11, Senators Clinton and Schumer marched into the Oval Office and told President Bush, "We need $20 billion to rebuild New York." Now, this was not a figure that came from any study; it was not arrived at by experts. Schumer later told *New York Daily News* that "we asked for it because we figured that's as much as we could get," and they were shocked when President Bush actually said yes. So where did this money go?

Turns out New York got $19 million for an "I Love New York"

advertising campaign. Robert De Niro got $3 million for a film festival—not what taxpayers thought their money was going to. They thought it was going to reconstruct the World Trade Center.

Goldman Sachs received millions of dollars in 9/11 federal money, despite the fact that they turn billions of dollars in profit every year. This isn't a struggling company that needs federal help. But they took the money and used it to build a forty-three-story headquarters right across from Ground Zero. And Hillary was there at the ribbon-cutting ceremony, taking credit for getting the money. So what's interesting about this story? Goldman Sachs is the second largest contributor to her campaign war chest. That's how Hillary works: "I give you federal money; you give me money for my campaign."

And whenever spending bills came up, Hillary hustled down to the Senate floor to make her positions clear. Bay Buchanan, former treasurer of the United States, tallied the numbers on Hillary's spending votes:

On the campaign trail, Hillary has attempted to project herself as a balanced budget person and very moderate. But take a look at her record as a senator. She's the number one spender in the Senate. After only a year in office, she was labeled the number one spender of taxpayer money by *National Review*. She sponsored or cosponsored 169 bills that would have increased spending by $24 billion, and not one bill that would have reduced spending.

Hillary also made some big promises to potential constituents during the 2000 New York Senate campaign. On a tour through the economically depressed upstate region, Hillary gave a big speech that must have brought hope to many. So we visited with New York policy analysts and residents to gauge their reaction to Hillary's campaign promises.

A JOBS PROMISE THAT WENT SOUTH—LITERALLY

Longtime New Yorker George Marlin is the author of *Squandered Opportunities* (St. Augustine Press, 2006)—a look at the dreadful situation New York finds itself in. Marlin recalls Hillary's promise vividly:

> Hillary Clinton came in and promised that if elected, she would create 200,000 jobs for upstate New York. It was one of the most irresponsible statements she ever made because (a) it proved that she had no clue what was wrong with upstate New York and (b) there's no way the federal government can deliver that.

Larry Kudlow agrees that it's hard for a senator to dictate job creation:

> Senators don't have any real power or authority to do that kind of thing. Should she have made the promise? Oh sure, that's what politicians do. That's what God put them on the earth to do, to make promises they can't keep.

Tony Blankley explains why Hillary made the promise:

> Some people say it was imprudent of her to make that promise. Politically, it was not. She shrewdly judged that she could make the promise to get the votes in, and then people would forget all about it. That's part of the Clinton method, which is: say what you need to say at any given moment, and rely on the lack of memory of the American public and support of the mainstream media to support that lack of memory.

Amanda Carpenter outlines the plan Hillary had to create these jobs:

Of her seven-point plan, only two points actually happened. One was providing Internet access to low-income communities; the other was providing money to hire lawyers to start enterprises. By the end of her first term, New York had experienced a net loss of thirty-six thousand jobs. Turns out, all the government money she threw at the problem didn't solve it. This must have been a sour pill for the unemployed of New York.

After her failure, a reporter asked her what happened. Her excuse was, "We certainly could have done it . . . if not for the Bush tax cuts." Huh? She takes no responsibility.

HOW HILLARY COULD HAVE GENUINELY FIXED NEW YORK

Newt Gingrich says the Bush tax cuts were the only hope upstate New York had of competing:

If New York State wasn't so burdened by heavy taxes, heavy union-ism, and heavy red tape, upstate New York would be doing dramatically better. The fact is, when you go around the country, the places in trouble are the places with strong union influence. They have high taxes. They have big governments. And they have lots of regulatory red tape. Every place that has low taxes, smaller governments, less red tape, and lesser union influence seems to be doing just fine. I think there's a hint there.

George Marlin believes the only real fix for New York's problems would be to unburden the state of taxes:

Fact is, the Bush tax cuts actually helped New York more than any other state in the nation. That's because any decline in the capital gains rate means more money goes into the state's bread and butter—

stock trading and investment banking deals, which in turn generate income tax for the state's coffers.

But Hillary wasn't about to deal with the tax structure! So instead, when she failed to create all the promised jobs, she became evasive and vague and ultimately blamed the Bush economic and tax policies for her failure, claiming that if we still had the Clinton policies, everything would have worked out. It was a ridiculous statement, but a lot of people bought it.

As the financial capital of the world, New York's economic health is very dependent on the capital gains tax rates. Larry Kudlow elaborates:

Senator Clinton voted against the financial district's interests when she voted against Bush's cuts in capital gains taxes. So I don't fault her for making the jobs promise. I fault her for making bad votes in the Senate against the very tax cuts that would have helped the state of New York.

Senator Clinton is running on a platform of "government investment," which is code for more government spending. And I think that's going to prove to be a very unpopular position. I'll give you an example:

Since [hurricane] Katrina, the government has thrown $120 billion at New Orleans. It is one of the great examples of the big-government, liberal-spending vision. But it has utterly failed New Orleans. Two years and $120 billion later, almost everyone agrees the city is in horrible shape.

But still Senator Clinton wants to send more money to New Orleans. She wants to send more money to different pockets in the United States. It makes for lousy economics, but it's all about politics to her. Parcel out favors to individual groups, get their votes, and move on. We're going to see a lot more of these government give-aways if Mrs. Clinton is elected president.

We can also expect Mrs. Clinton as president to allow the Bush tax cuts to expire in 2010. If that happens, you're going to see a problem in investment and in the stock market and business later on. The Bush tax cuts were aimed at creating new incentives to invest and save after the Internet bubble and stock market plunge that he inherited in 2001.

So Hillary will slow the economy.

If you raise taxes across the board, you're going to do harm to the economy. How much harm? I wouldn't want to predict. We'll have to see what it looks like at that time. But you're certainly not going to create the kind of jobs you want to create.

If Hillary lets Bush's tax cuts expire, will only businesses be affected, or will individual consumers pay as well? George Marlin paints a picture of the pressures New York faces with its tax structure:

New York has the highest state and local tax burden of any state in the nation. Other states have higher income taxes. Other states have higher property taxes. But when you put the whole picture together, New York State has the highest taxes per capita in the nation. So the first step in fixing New York is to attack all of the government programs that cost taxpayers so much money.

A good example is the situation in healthcare. In upstate New York, the fastest growing job sector is healthcare jobs paid for by the government [in other words, by taxpayers]. Between 1980 and 2004, employment in healthcare jobs leaped 75 percent in New York, compared to a 7 percent increase nationwide. How does this affect the overall economy?

All it does is keep empty hospitals and health facilities open to the public, whether they're being used or not. . . . It destroys the economic base of the area because tax dollars are being used to fund it, and to keep funding those jobs, you have to keeping raising taxes. It's a treadmill to oblivion.

The bottom line, says Amanda Carpenter, is

Hillary has never seen a tax she doesn't like. She says she is more fiscally responsible now, but that sounds like an excuse to get back into your wallet.

HILLARY TO AMERICA: "GET READY TO SACRIFICE!"

In a rare moment of candor at George Washington University on June 4, 2007, Hillary told her assembled admirers, "We have to build a political consensus. And that requires people giving up a little bit of their own turf, in order to create this common ground. . . . And that means something has to be taken away from some people."

There was consensus among our film's participants that this speech captured the real Hillary we would see in office. As Tony Blankley says,

Hillary has tried of late to portray herself as a free-market centrist. But in a private meeting with no cameras present, she said the government should take property away from people and distribute it where it needs to go. We have to take these as hints of the true left-wing Hillary. And if these instincts were given free rein in the Oval Office, we can only imagine what kind of confiscatory and oppressive nanny-state policies would weigh over the American people.

When Hillary talks about taking revenues for the common good, she is assuming that you can keep taxing the productive activity of individuals and companies and keep extracting more and more wealth out of them. The history of the last one hundred years has shown just the opposite.

That is why the richest individuals in the world come from countries with free markets. And that is why Socialist and Communist regimes of the world have ended up giving less to everybody.

Hillary's egalitarian theories have manifestly failed. Her husband recognized as much, which is why he chose to become a free-market Democrat. It's revealing that her old instincts are stronger than her powers of recall on her husband's policies.

Hillary may in fact be politically much further to the left than her husband, in the view of Larry Kudlow:

Hillary's "common good" means "government." It means Washington. She is opposed to the ownership class President Bush talks about. She is opposed to the free-enterprise entrepreneurship President Reagan talked about. She wants government to be in control.

If you take it to its logical extreme, Governor Romney is right. She sounds more like Karl Marx than Adam Smith. I think Hillary's economic policies are going to be a big issue in this campaign. Who do folks want to run the economy? Do they want the market, or do they want the government? We have fought this battle in American politics for twenty-five years, ever since Reagan was elected. And we will fight it again. I think she's going to be very vulnerable on this key question.

Bob Novak agrees, and suggests what could happen if Hillary is elected and Democrats retain control of Congress:

It is true that the model of a Hillary Clinton presidency, much more than her husband, would be expanded social welfare. The basic message to the American people would be: "If you're having a tough time, the government is here to help."

Now about half the American people don't believe government should help them, and half believe the government should help them. The former tends to vote Republican, the latter Democratic — that's politics today.

With Hillary, we get bigger government.

In fact, we don't know what programs Bill Clinton would have pursued if there had been a Democratic Congress. For six of his eight years, he faced Republican control of Congress. If Hillary comes into office on a Democratic surge, with a working Democratic majority in the House and Senate, you're going to see things her husband couldn't do. And that involves increased spending and taxation, and redistribution of income.

I don't think there's any doubt that there's going to be a lot more spending and a lot more taxation, and that the seemingly simple way to pay for all this is to tax the rich. It's a Democratic disease. Of course, when you tax the rich and redistribute income, there are always some unintended consequences.

One, you hurt the economy and depress investment.

Two, you can't just tax the rich without hitting a lot of middle income people.

Hillary just doesn't trust individual Americans to make their own choices, and that's at odds with the thinking of many Americans, says Michael Medved:

One of the questions I ask people on my radio show is: where did we get this idea that tax money collected from the paychecks of bus drivers and plumbers and janitors all over the country should go to finance things like students at Yale? Where does this idea come from? It's absurd!

This is exactly the wrong kind of welfare, and it is what Clintonism leads to. It's Robin Hood in reverse—taking from the hardworking poor to give to people who, if they're not rich already, are going to be rich.

This "Robin Hood in reverse" theme was echoed by Dick Armey:

At least Robin Hood stole from the rich and gave to the poor. How many government programs actually steal from the poor to subsidize the privileged? I'll give you an example. When I taught night classes, I saw people who worked all day, earning a living, supporting their family and paying taxes. Now when I taught day classes, what did I see? People who were not married, who were unemployed, who had government loans or Pell Grants that were paid for by whom?

By the taxes of those night-school students. All too often the most hardworking among us are being overburdened with taxation to subsidize the lives of the more privileged among us.

Later in her "common good" speech Hillary added that "fairness doesn't just happen, it requires the right government policies." This tells us what kind of economic model Hillary subscribes to, says Newt Gingrich, as well as her thoughts about the individual American:

Senator Clinton represents an almost West German socialist model. Willie Brandt was one of the great heroes of her generation on the Left, and like him, I don't think she trusts people to make decisions about fairness. She thinks that if you give politicians and bureaucrats that power, somehow they'll be able to make those decisions better for you.

WHAT GRADE HAS SENATOR CLINTON EARNED?

Edward Klein gives her relatively high marks:

When Hillary became senator, many people thought she would be a disaster because she had no experience in playing nice with others. But she was well coached, and she was smart enough to win over the "bulls" of the Senate. She's been brilliant at that. She's become the consummate Washington insider.

Michael Medved gives her a mixed review:

I often ask people to look at Hillary and just think, *She could be the next leader of the Free World.* Now, if she hadn't been married to Bill Clinton, what has she accomplished in her life that would lead you to believe that she should be the most powerful person in the country?

She's raised a nice daughter, she's held her marriage together under trying circumstances, but what has she accomplished? I know her colleagues in the Senate think well of her.

But what enterprise has she led successfully?

I've talked to senators—Democrats and Republicans—who say she's good to work with. And in Congress, there are some hot dogs who are there just to show off. She's not like that. You can work with her. But having said that, she hasn't had a dazzling Senate career.

Soon she will have had eight years in the Senate and sixty years on this planet—where are the footprints?

Jeff Gerth says her grade depends on which Hillary shows up:

There are two Hillarys. There's one Hillary who gets high grades. She goes to hearings; she does her homework; she comes home late at night with two hundred pages of briefing books, she digests them, and she's up at the crack of dawn well prepared and articulate. She has paid attention to her constituents. She got herself onto the Armed Services Committee, became a student of military affairs, became close to a number of people in the military. That Hillary gets high marks.

But then there's the other Hillary who when she encounters a bump in the road, she dissembles. She plays fast and loose with the facts. No longer does she reach out to her opponent, she lashes out. She hunkers down. That Hillary doesn't get high marks at all.

So the real question is: which Hillary would we elect president?

One of Hillary's big heroes is Eleanor Roosevelt. And in the course of our reporting, we uncovered a radio show that Eleanor Roosevelt did in 1934. She was asked during this show, "When will a woman become president?"

Her answer boiled down to one sentence: when a majority of the American people have trust and confidence in the integrity of that woman. That's the challenge Hillary faces. As I said, there are two Hillarys, and only one of them inspires trust and confidence.

George Marlin grades Hillary in view of how New York has fared during her term as its senator:

We're seeing an unprecedented flight out of upstate New York because of the lack of economic opportunities there. More people fleeing the state than any other state in the nation. The hardest hit is twenty-to-thirty-year-olds. The average person who graduates from college in upstate New York moves away—there are no jobs. With this flight of young people, certain areas in upstate New York are becoming deserted.

New numbers just came out. From March 2000 to March 2006, roughly Hillary's term, one million New Yorkers moved out of the state.

Upstate has been hit hardest. Long Island has also been heavily hit. Because of the tax structure, property values are rising dramatically, and the property tax is going up relative to that. People can't afford housing.

Upstate New York is broken. In 1960, Buffalo had 800,000 residents. Today it has 250,000 residents with little hope. Buffalo has 20,000 vacant single family homes. The surrounding area of Erie County has 35,000 additional vacant homes. Grandpa dies. [The family] can't sell it. They can't afford it. They walk away from it. That's how economically devastated Buffalo is. In fact, three years ago the mayor of Buffalo called for the dissolution of the city. Can you imagine things getting so bad the sitting mayor just says, "Let's end the city"?

In Oswego County so far in 2007, seven dairy farms have closed. [The farmers are] just walking away and mailing the keys to the bank. I met a county legislator in Oswego County who told me she is turning over her Social Security check to her son each month to help keep his dairy farm open. That's how desperate it is.

While the nation witnessed a great housing boom in the last ten years, Oswego County home prices dropped 43 percent. Rural areas in New York State are going to be completely vacant in a few short years.

Perhaps worst of all is the "bright flight" we're seeing. We've got young kids coming out of colleges and then leaving because they cannot find jobs. In upstate New York, you have four in ten young people simply leaving the state.

We visited upstate New York to ask Senator Clinton's constituents what they thought of her performance. Here is a selection of our interviews:

BOB HASENOEHRL

I own a trucking company here in western New York. In 2000, I was invited to attend a meeting with Hillary at the Chamber of Commerce.

I figured it would be a great time to meet the first lady and listen to what she had to say. She's a very charismatic speaker. She promised to deliver two hundred thousand jobs in the western New York area.

I'd be happy to know we got two thousand jobs. Things have gotten a lot worse since then. The promises weren't lived up to at all. Our trucking firm is continually moving folks out of the area. We just had another company close up—lost another six hundred to seven hundred jobs.

Every day we have somebody moving out of the area. Selling their homes, devastated. Most of them are moving south to the Carolinas. We're losing our young people when they graduate from college. We're losing a lot of retirees because they can't afford to live here.

CHARLIE LUBERGER

I'm a farmer in Smyrna, New York. We'd like to see Senator Clinton up here more. She tends to spend most of her time down state. Sometimes we feel forgotten up here. Dairy farming is the engine of the community, at least where I live. And if the farmer isn't doing well, then it goes right down through the feed, the seed dealer, and all the people that support the farm.

Interest in ethanol has driven up the price of feed and driven up the price of fuel—it's not helping the bottom line. We'd like to see Senator Clinton up here taking a position. She's wavered on the issue—I think that's the way she works. I think she has good attributes. But the attribute I don't like about her is how she changes her opinion based upon the polls and what's politically advantageous.

MICHAEL MORRILL

Hillary's policies toward business, especially small business in my case, have given me no benefit at all. If anything, there are such restrictions. Hillary Clinton for president? No. Is that simple enough for you?

JIM PARKER

Hillary is a typical politician. Whatever the survey shows she should be doing, she's doing. And it's not just her; it's the entire structure of New York State politics. We have an overweight of government. When government is the major employer, that's completely out of focus. It's not the American dream; it's upside down. And nobody has the courage to get rid of this mess of people collecting pensions. Hillary Clinton and her husband are in that category. Public service is really the wrong thing to call what they're doing. They're serving themselves primarily.

I'd like to ask Hillary Clinton what she really knows about the Iraq War. I was in the Persian Gulf as an officer in the navy. We are there doing the right thing. We're making progress. These Democrats—they just knock it down. It's not fair to our troops. It's not fair to our country. They just ought to shut their mouths.

KEITH LEWICKI

Running a business in New York is a losing proposition. You see people leaving constantly. I'm married, and my wife has a good job, but I go to Florida for four or five months a year to work—and that's where I make my money. And I don't think Hillary is going to do anything about it. One person can't anyway. It's not just her. It's New York. I mean, they're just driving business out of the state. Go south. That's the rule of thumb.

MARSHALL BROWN

I've been running G&B Farms by myself for twenty years. The last few years have been toughest. We lose money every month. I've borrowed and sold assets just to stay in business.

Three years ago, Hillary Clinton came to Oswego County. She said she had a plan for the dairy industry. Like all her plans, she never gives any specifics except to say, "It's going to make everything all wonderful for us." Two years after she gave her "I got a plan" speech, the price of milk dropped to the same level it was in 1979, and I'm losing my ass.

Oswego County lost seven dairy farmers just this spring due to the economic circumstances. Agriculture is New York State's largest industry. Dairy farming is the largest segment of that. I don't know if Hillary was told that when she got off the plane. If I could ask Hillary one question, it would be: "Senator Clinton, when you came to Oswego County and you said you had a plan for the dairy industry three years ago, was that plan to put us all on food stamps?"

7

STRUCK TWICE BY TERRORISM: A FAMILY'S MESSAGE FOR HILLARY

Terrorism has twice shattered the Connor family of New Jersey—once in 1975 when FALN terrorists murdered Frank Connor, and again in 2001 when al-Qaeda terrorists murdered Steve Schlag. Now for the first time we hear the story of Hillary's role in excusing these terrorist murders, as told by Joe Connor:

> Fraunces Tavern occupies an extraordinary place in American history. It's where a secret organization of American patriots met to map out the American Revolution. It's where George Washington bid farewell to his officers at the end of war. It's also where my father, Frank Connor, was murdered at 1:30 in the afternoon on January 24, 1975.
>
> Dad worked for the Morgan Guarantee Trust Company. He started there right out of high school when his mother, also an Irish immigrant and a cleaning lady there, got him the job. Grandma was very excited that her son got a job in a very prestigious bank, because he would get a free lunch every day. That was a big thing for them.
>
> My dad was only thirty-three, a father of two—my brother Tom and me. He was a decent, honest family man. On that day, he

was looking forward to coming home to celebrate my brother's eleventh and my ninth birthdays. It was going to be a big family event for us.

Even before the bomb exploded, Mom had premonitions and knew something was wrong. She'd called his office that day, and when he didn't pick up, she immediately knew he was in the bomb blast. It wasn't until his coworkers came by that we knew for sure. I was a little nine-year-old, and one of the guys picked me up, and I just started punching him in the back—not knowing what else to do.

Not a day went by that we didn't think about my father—about his life, not his death. We tried not to dwell on that, or on the terrorists. We thought about how we were going to stay together as a family and succeed. My brother and I have done okay. We went to college, have families of our own, good jobs. A lot of credit goes to my mom and my grandmother—they were always looking forward.

But on that day, I lost more than my father; I lost a nine-year-old's innocence and the notion that "life is good."

Rick Hahn is now a retired FBI agent. When terrorism struck lower Manhattan in 1975, Mr. Hahn was mobilized there on the street to investigate and bring the terrorists to justice. He is the foremost authority on FALN (the Spanish initials for Armed Forces of National Liberation). Hahn explains:

FALN was newly formed, completely clandestine. We had no idea who the actual members were. It wasn't until 1976 when a safe house was stumbled onto by Chicago police that we identified any of their members. It took years to find out their goal, which was to break Puerto Rico away from the U.S. and turn it into a socialist nation.

On that cold January day, the bomber apparently came into the dining room of Fraunces Tavern. Witnesses remember seeing a man carrying a large duffel bag. One of the waiters was about to tell him to leave. But he stepped back outside first, and then left the bomb in an adjacent stairwell. Fifteen minutes later, it blew. The table closest to the stairwell, where Frank Connor and two others sat, was obliterated. Upstairs, a man was killed by a nail that shot up through the floor. Much of the dining room was destroyed, and fifty-eight other diners were wounded. They used an estimated twelve tons of dynamite. Had the bomb been placed in the room, there would have been many casualties.

At first, the police didn't respond because they thought it was a gas explosion and a matter for the public works department. Nobody imagined that this could be a bombing, in broad daylight, in a restaurant in New York City. It simply was not the sort of thing that happened in America.

After a thorough search, the crime scene guys found pieces of a propane tank—a trademark of FALN bombings. By 3 p.m., a communiqué had been recovered just a few blocks from the tavern. The FALN claimed credit, saying they wanted to kill capitalist-imperialist pigs.

And they were serious. From when they began to 1982, the FALN were responsible for 107 bombings in New York, Chicago, and Washington. They invaded the campaign headquarters of Carter, Mondale, and Bush. They put people down on the floor at gunpoint, stole lists of delegates to conventions, and sent them threatening letters. They invaded a National Guard Armory in Wisconsin—trying to steal weapons and explosives. They were the most prolific terrorist group in history.

In the years that followed the loss of his father, Joe Connor studied up on the FALN and followed their activities:

Yes, FALN held the dubious distinction of being the most prolific terrorist group in American history until al-Qaeda. Fortunately they were captured and convicted of seditious conspiracy. At the time of their sentencing they remained unrepentant, however, and even publicly threatened to kill the judge. They were terrible people. But justice had been served. They were in jail. The bombings stopped, never to be worried about again—until President Clinton pardoned these very FALN terrorists.

I remember the day—it was in August 1999. I had been to the zoo with my wife and our two kids, and when we came home, the phone was ringing. My wife answered, and I could tell by her expression that something was terribly wrong. I said, "He pardoned them, didn't he?" There had been rumors.

CLINTON PARDONS MOST PROLIFIC
TERRORISTS IN U.S. HISTORY

At the time he granted clemency (often used interchangeably with "pardon"), Bill Clinton claimed that the FALN were not violent criminals and that they deserved a second chance. FBI agent Rick Hahn's job had been to track and capture these supposedly "non-violent" terrorists:

All of the FALN terrorists had been convicted of conspiracy to overthrow the country, possession of explosives, armed robbery, bombings. One FALN member did cooperate with the FBI, so we know just how violent they really were. His name was Freddie Mendez, and he told us how he and fellow FALN went into Carter-Mondale headquarters and put guns in the faces of campaign workers; how they went into the armory in Wisconsin and put those people down on the floor and threatened their lives; how they placed bombs around the country.

In addition, we had closed-circuit video of these FALN terrorists building bomb-firing triggers and cleaning their weapons. To call these people nonviolent is ludicrous fiction. What's more, at the time of their sentencing, one of the FALN members said to the judge, "If I could, I'd put you down right now."

Yet they were handed clemency and not even required to cooperate with law enforcement to help solve the string of unsolved FALN crimes. I know of no other instance where criminals were given clemency, or even leniency on their sentences, without cooperating with law enforcement in some way. Yet the FALN didn't cooperate. They mocked the court even as they were set free by Clinton.

So why were they set free?

The Justice Department publicly opposed the pardons. A long line of people appeared before Congress opposing the pardons. So why would Bill Clinton pardon convicted terrorists, releasing them onto the streets of America? Joe Connor has also studied the Clintons' motives:

Why would the president grant these clemencies, when he had three thousand other clemency petitions pending, when his own FBI and Department of Justice argued strenuously against the clemencies, unless there was a clear beneficiary?

The Clintons never did anything that wasn't politically calculated. So we have to look at how releasing these terrorists would help the Clintons in some way. Well, Hillary was planning to run for Senate in New York. There are 3.5 million Puerto Rican, Hispanic voters in that state. It would appear they were trying to curry favor with these voters.

Apparently the Clintons decided that if they had to pardon a few terrorists to get Hillary elected, then the ends justified the means. We don't know for sure, because the Clintons have stonewalled when asked about this. But the man who knows them best, the man who was there when the cynical Clinton calculus was spinning unchecked, the man named Dick Morris, offers a concise analysis of what happened:

> Hillary's biggest problem in running for the Senate was that she wasn't a New Yorker. How was she going to appeal to the ethnic groups of New York, the biggest group being people of Puerto Rican extraction?
>
> In September 1999, in the middle of her Senate campaign, she was approached by city councilman Jose Rivera, a spokesman for the Hispanic community in New York. He gave her a packet urging the pardoning of the FALN terrorists.
>
> Two days later, the pardons were granted. Obviously this helped Hillary win the Hispanic vote. Obviously she asked Bill to grant the pardons. And obviously when she says she knows nothing about these pardons, she's not telling the truth.

What was most amazing about these pardons was the fact that the FALN terrorists at first rejected them. The government's clemency agreement stipulated that (1) the FALN couldn't associate with other felons and (2) they had to renounce violence as a means to political ends. But they refused to accept these terms of release. They were martyrs to their cause. They rejected the government's offer, as Joe Connor recounts:

> The FALN terrorists said publicly that they'd rather stay in jail than renounce their terrorist agenda. Clinton released them anyway.
>
> Clinton put his own political agenda above my father's life! My father was an honest family man being used as a political pawn by people who didn't have his decency, didn't have his values.
>
> Bill Clinton isn't half the man my father was. Hillary Clinton

isn't half the man my father was. This was an absolute kick in the stomach to my family. And as a family, we all agreed to make people aware of what was going on. It was a quiet news time. Congress was out of session. So we contacted the news media and tried to raise awareness, and it worked! People got furious about what Bill Clinton had done. Hillary had been supporting the clemencies. But when she saw it becoming a political problem for her, she instantly backtracked.

People of Puerto Rican origin in New York don't support terrorism. They don't want people like Frank Connor murdered. And even in Puerto Rico, less than 4 percent of the people had voted for independence from the United States.

The power of the pardon, which is an extraordinarily powerful tool, is the one unchecked power that the president is given. In fact, in *The Federalist Papers*, Alexander Hamilton wrote that no president would abuse that power lest he be thought conniving. Alexander Hamilton never envisioned Bill and Hillary Clinton.

Rick Hahn sees the Clintons' actions as more than cruel political calculus:

There is no un-ringing the bell. Releasing the FALN members sent a message that the United States is willing to negotiate with terrorists, is willing to roll over and capitulate. Any terrorist that knows anything about the FALN pardons, whether it's Osama bin Laden himself or Khalid Sheikh Mohammed, would conclude that they could through political means obtain release from prison from the United States.

Joe Connor sees the irony in Clinton's releasing the FALN terrorists almost two years to the day before 9/11:

Clinton has insisted again and again that he was hard at work fighting terrorism during this time. These pardons speak the truth about Clinton's mind-set toward terrorism—they were granted almost two years to the day before 9/11, at a time when Clinton was supposedly hard at work chasing terrorists.

As well, while we don't know what kind of encouragement the FALN pardons might have given other terrorists who were watching; it surely didn't discourage them.

Did the Clintons directly abet future terrorist activities by selfishly pardoning the FALN terrorists? Possibly; possibly not. But the forthcoming story suggests that yes, the Clintons sent a clear message to terrorists that America was easy prey.

9/11'S DEEPER MEANING TO THE CONNOR FAMILY

As for the Connor family, they would soon learn the cost of being soft on terrorism when they were struck tragically a second time on 9/11. This time Joe Connor was standing in his office at 60 Wall Street, and he watched the second plane hit the tower where his cousin Steve Schlag worked. Joe recalls the moment:

When I saw the first fireball, I thought it was a bomb. Then when I saw the second plane coming south down Manhattan, I knew it was January 24 all over again. I tried to call my cousin Steve, who worked for Cantor Fitzgerald, but couldn't get through.

I called my brother Tom, who agreed that it was terrorism and we had to get out fast. Others were staying. But we didn't know how many more planes were coming. I was not going to orphan my kids, the way it happened to me.

It was the thought of my family, of having the same thing happen to them as happened to me, growing up fatherless and always the pain—that was the motivation to get out. My dad was sitting at a table and had no chance to defend himself. I had a chance.

When we finally got home on September 11, my brother and I drove up to Franklin Lakes to where cousin Steve lived. The entire family drove in and waited, hoping for a miracle, knowing none would come. It was eerily similar to the scene at my house years earlier, when we had waited for word of my father.

I later took the train to the place where Steve's car was parked— somebody had to retrieve the car. It was horrible seeing it there, where Steve left it that morning. It was the same place my dad had parked in 1975, the same train station. It was hard to imagine that terrorism had struck our family twice.

Joe Connor doesn't dwell on the past, but he firmly believes we should learn from it. He feels that some of us have become complacent about the terrorist threat, and others of us have let our feelings about the current administration override our memories of the devastation rained down on 9/11:

Look at how quick people who've never been touched by terrorism are to limit law enforcement's ability to go after terrorists. Before 9/11, who would have thought that a few guys with razors could have taken down the World Trade Center? That would have been laughable! Now we see that same naiveté and denial when, say, actual terrorist cells are found operating on native soil. We are hearing from left-wing politicians that these terror cells don't pose any threat, or if they do we can't infringe on anyone's civil liberties by aggressively monitoring them, God forbid!

As the head of the congressional committee that investigated all the last-minute Clinton pardons—from the FALN, to tax evader Marc

Rich to the other felons, drug dealers, and con artists that Clinton released—Congressman Dan Burton had his hands full. He remembers the feeling of a scandal-du-jour that was the Clinton term of office:

> The FALN terrorists were the worst of the political pardons, but far from the only pardons. In his final days in office, Bill Clinton pardoned dozens of dangerous criminals. It was all about getting a political edge or getting a wad of cash.
>
> Hillary Clinton was an integral part of the decision-making process. Her fingerprints were all over everything.
>
> Of course when our oversight committee tried to get information from senior White House officials, it was like pulling teeth. Some claimed executive privilege. Others were forced to come up to testify, but they took the Fifth Amendment, fled the country, or had a sudden bout of memory loss.
>
> Bill Clinton was the epitome of the political animal. He was very corrupt; he was also very gregarious and likeable. Hillary is a lot less likable, but just as corrupt. Having them back would really set us back.

HILLARY'S ROLE IN PARDONING DRUG DEALERS

Dick Morris asks us to look beyond the pardons that were, in fact, made by Bill Clinton and look at the pardons that must be laid solely at Hillary's doorstep:

> The thing Hillary has to answer for, and never has, is how her brother Hugh Rodham was paid $200,000 to [obtain a] pardon [for] Carlos Vignali—the top crack dealer and cocaine supplier in Minnesota. Hillary's brother also got $200,000 to [obtain a] pardon [for] another felon. And her other brother got $102,000 to [obtain a] pardon [for] the owner of a carnival.

Hillary claims she didn't know anything about these pardons. But is that credible?

Hugh Rodham, who was pushing the Vignali pardon, lived in the White House during the month of December when these pardons were cooked up. He was constantly pressuring Bill Clinton to grant these pardons. Do you think it's (a) credible that Bill didn't know that the guy was getting paid for it, and (b) he didn't talk to his wife when he was granting a pardon at her brother's request? I don't think that's credible.

Either way, it's outrageous behavior to pardon a guy who sold crack to kids—simply because your brother got money for it.

Then there was the New York Hassidic pardon. Noting that it is illegal to offer something of value in return for a vote, Dick Morris asks you to judge whether Hillary Clinton broke the law:

In 1999, four leaders of the so-called "New Square Hassidic Community" were sentenced to two-to-six years in federal prison for bilking taxpayers out of $40 million. They had invented 1,500 phantom students, applied for scholarship aid, and pocketed the money. The next year Hillary visited New Square during her campaign and met with the leadership of the community. They asked her to arrange a meeting with her husband to see about granting clemency to the four felons.

The community voted for Hillary Clinton 1,400 to 3 after virtually all other Hassidic communities went against Hillary.

Shortly after the election, on December 22, there was a meeting in the White House with Bill and Hillary and the leaders of the New Square community. A month later the pardons were granted.

Coincidence?

You decide.

8

WHEN I WORKED FOR THE CLINTONS . . .

For our film and this book, we contacted quite a few people who had worked with or for the Clintons over the years, eager to get their first-hand perspectives on both of the Clintons—primarily Hillary. The response we received did not surprise us, though it sure frustrated us.

Understandably, most of the people we wanted to speak to are liberal partisans and were not interested in cooperating—even though we welcomed their point of view. Others expressed an interest in speaking with us, but when we called back to schedule a convenient time, they suddenly became unavailable. We saw that as part of a larger pattern with the Clintons and found it regrettable, but we understood.

We did speak to two of those Clinton associates—one now in jail, one facing sentencing as we spoke. Those interviews form the basis of chapter 1.

We also spoke with two people who found themselves on the receiving end of the Clintons' politics of personal destruction. Those interviews are chapters 2 and 3. Many of the participants in our film and book were touched in some way by the Clintons' politics of personal destruction. And three of those people managed to survive relatively unscathed, though with stories that should be required listening in the election ahead.

GARY ALDRICH

As the senior FBI agent assigned to the White House during the Clinton administration, Gary Aldrich was so appalled by what he saw that he wrote *Unlimited Access: An FBI Agent Inside the Clinton White House* (Regnery, 1996). As with others who found themselves close to the Clintons and duty-bound to write about their misdeeds, Gary Aldrich has been reflexively attacked by the liberal media. But when you hear Gary Aldrich's story, you hear the ominous ring of truth:

It was very exciting being an FBI agent assigned to the White House. It was the best possible assignment an agent like me could achieve. I knew I'd be working with high-quality people. I was one of two senior agents. We had our own office, our set of keys, passes that would allow us to go anywhere.

My principal responsibility at the start of any new administration was to vet candidates for employment to determine whether they were suitable for federal posts and top-secret clearances to work near the president. The purpose of all this, of course, was to protect national security—not just the secrets that flow through the White House on a daily basis, but also the physical security of the people and the place.

The acronym for the FBI clearance process had long been SPIN, but after the Clintons came to town, the word *spin* took on a new meaning. So the FBI was forced to change the name! But it worked like this:

An applicant would be asked to complete a number of lengthy forms, detailing information going all the way back to high school days. There was also an interview to drill down on qualifications, suitability, and integrity. It was crucial for us to know if applicants were telling the truth and if they could be trusted with sensitive information. A lie on the forms or a lie told to an FBI agent constituted a federal felony.

We would interview college professors, look at grade point averages, and get transcripts of their schooling. We also went to previous employers to determine that they were not fluffing their résumés. We talked to former supervisors and coworkers in search of serious problems we should know about.

We were looking for a "general sense" of the person. Any one small matter might not be a disqualifier. However, if we saw a pattern of dishonesty, failure to meet financial obligations, difficulty working well with others, emotional problems, then we would look deeper into that behavior to see if there was a serious character flaw.

The final hiring decision is always made by the president and his staff. They can override any recommendations that are made by the agencies. However, in my experience at the White House, the recommendations of the FBI and the Secret Service had always been heeded.

CLINTONS NOT LIKE PAST ADMINISTRATIONS
Gary Aldrich continues:

With the Clintons, as with all new administrations, we were expecting an avalanche of paperwork from thousands of new employee candidates. But no paperwork came. We had extra staff on board to handle the influx of new people. But January 20 came and went, and the White House gates were thrown open to all kinds of people whose backgrounds were unknown to us.

As the FBI agent tasked with the security of the president, this made me feel very uncomfortable. We made numerous attempts to talk with anybody who would listen to allow us to conduct our investigations. The response was less than satisfying. When we asked why the paperwork was not forthcoming, Clinton staffers told us our investigations wouldn't matter because regardless of what turned up, they would have their jobs at the White House anyway.

That attitude concerned us, especially when we found people who had failed their investigations. Despite our recommendations to remove them because they were a security risk, they remained employed. In fact, some of them actually mocked us and said, "No matter what you turn up in the investigation, we'll be here long after you are gone."

Certainly the Clintons were entitled to run the White House the way they saw fit, not the way I saw fit. But there are a great many threats on the president's life from people who are unhinged, unhappy, whatever. If something happens to the president, our nation could be threatened. So Secret Service agents and FBI agents take security very seriously.

Then look at what was happening at the start of the Clinton term:

President Bush had sent troops into Kuwait to drive out the Iraqi invaders. Based on that action, Middle Eastern terrorists had threatened the life of the president. We worried that the White House would be a terror target. We also knew that terrorists tried to kill former president Bush when he traveled to Kuwait. So it worried us intensely when the Clintons just laughed off these threats.

WIDESPREAD ABUSE OF ILLEGAL DRUGS

In our investigations into Clinton staffers, we discovered that one in four was using illegal drugs. These are not my numbers, by the way. Those numbers were recited under oath by the Secret Service to congressional committees. Now our concern was not people who experimented with marijuana in college. Our concern was people in their midthirties or older who continued to use drugs on a regular basis as a lifestyle.

Beyond drugs, we had a multitude of offenses ranging from wife beating to failure to pay income taxes. One Clinton employee used the White House Credit Union to conduct a check-kiting fraud!

When we discussed our findings with White House counsel's office, they basically patted us on the head and condescendingly told us we should relax and lighten up; this was not the Bush or the Reagan administration; these were new kinds of folks coming in, folks who were younger, and clearly there was a cultural gap and an age gap that we old fogies couldn't possibly understand.

There was also the excuse that some of these folks were up from the poor South so their standards might be different than ours.

I obviously had a hard time believing their explanations because having worked in state, federal, local governments my entire FBI career, I found it hard to believe the Clinton administration could not find quality people to work in the White House.

It wasn't too long before the newspapers in town became aware of the problem. And the White House was asked to explain why so many people were working there without security clearances—after an entire year!

Clinton's spokesman tried to suggest that there weren't many non-secure employees, just a couple of oversights. Then when the media pressed harder, the explanation was changed to, "Well, there may be more than just a few, but there are reasonable explanations." Then the news came out that there were literally hundreds of people working at the White House, after a full year, without security clearances.

ACTIVITIES THAT MADE YOU SHAKE YOUR HEAD

There were several examples of things that made you say, "I can't believe this is the White House."

We had a number of stoned thieves. There was this big announcement that the Clinton White House would be more technologically advanced than all others. And in fact, they brought in a lot of laptop computers for the staff. But they couldn't keep enough laptops. They were going out the door faster than they could bring them in!

When the Secret Service discovered who was stealing laptops, the thieves claimed they were being discriminated against; they were minorities, and they were supposedly being singled out. In other words, their defense was, "We're not the only thieves around here; why pick on us?"

Another example, a small but a telling one, was the White House cafeteria at noon hour. You would see people eating their food in line while they were waiting to pay for it. Why were they doing that? Because the food was weighed by the pound. You would think people would be honest enough to pay for their yogurt and french fries. But not these people.

Then you had people writing bad checks to the Secret Service Gift Shop. You see, the Secret Service has a gift shop in the basement where they sell things like golf balls and coffee mugs with the White House logo on them. Very nice items. And all the profits from this gift shop go to the Secret Service Widows & Orphans Fund. Every staffer has this explained to them. So they knew they were stealing money from widows and orphans. It was outrageous!

HILLARY'S ROLE IN HIRING SUCH LOSERS

Through the course of our background investigations, we would learn everything about an individual—including their relationship with the Clintons. It didn't take long to discover that Hillary Clinton was involved in the selection of most of the key White House people. Plus she would sit in on the final interviews.

So it's safe to say that Hillary was disregarding FBI recommendations. We were told by counsel's office that certain individuals were coming to work for the White House whether we liked or not. One of those individuals was Craig Livingstone.

Livingstone was hired to work with the FBI and the Secret Service to make sure that we did our job properly. That was the oddest thing to us in light of all we'd seen with the Clintons and in light of his qualifications. The people who had held this position before Livingstone had long-term experience with personnel processing and national security issues. He came in totally green.

We care about Livingstone for several reasons—the first being the sleazy injustice that came to be known as Filegate.

Filegate was a situation where Livingstone and his staff found a clever way to request classified FBI files on previous administrations' senior officials. They were able to get files on senior Bush and Reagan officials that they had no legal reason to request and the FBI would not have released if they understood what was going on.

Of course the Clintons claimed the whole thing was a bureaucratic snafu, and unfortunately the FBI director backed them up, so nothing came of this. But more than a thousand classified records were sent to the Clinton White House, and for what purpose?

For spying on political enemies? For finding information to use against political enemies? This information wasn't useful for anything else!

When Hillary Clinton was deposed under oath, she claimed to not even know Livingstone's first name! This is at odds with sworn testimony of other Clinton officials who overheard her in the hallways referring to Livingstone by his first name, Craig.

Of course by this time, I didn't believe anything coming out of the mouths of the Clintons, either Bill or Hillary. We were seeing so much dishonesty, dissembling, and spin. It was difficult to tell the truth from the fiction.

HILLARY'S ASSAULT ON THE TRAVEL OFFICE
THE MOST DESPICABLE

Gary Aldrich was particularly disgusted at Billy Dale's treatment:

Another example of Clintonian corruption involved the White House Travel Office. My partner and I had previously done investigations on these employees and determined that they were honest individuals, qualified to work in the White House. We were convinced these were good quality people. We had never heard an allegation of any kind ever made against them.

But suddenly they were fired and accused of serious wrongdoing, which, if proven, could send them to federal penitentiary.

The head of the Travel Office, Billy Dale, was one of the unsung heroes, the good-hearted souls who take positions in the federal government and work every day, diligently, loyal to whichever administration happens to be in power. Billy was not ashamed to say that he was a Democrat, that he had voted for Bill Clinton (the first time).

But they fired him, humiliated him publicly, accused him of serious wrongdoing, conducted a Federal Grand Jury investigation on him, and indicted him. When his case finally came to trial, all kinds of reporters and previous administration officials came to testify on his behalf. It took the jury only two hours to find him not guilty on all charges.

The Travel Office experience taught me how powerful politicians could misuse law enforcement authority almost whimsically. That's what this was. There weren't any serious allegations against Billy Dale. But because the first lady ordered an investigation, it had to take place and charges had to be brought. That scared me. In my twenty-six years in the FBI, I had never seen such wanton abuse of power.

(Our complete interview with Billy Dale is in chapter 3.)

THE DAY-TO-DAY EXPERIENCE OF WORKING WITH HILLARY

Former FBI Agent Aldrich says that Hillary Clinton had a low tolerance for any kind of small talk:

> She had an almost zealotlike focus on her political issues and an inability to hear the opinions of anybody else. What bothered me most was the way she treated the staff.
>
> If anyone on the permanent staff displeased her for any reason, they could count on being punished. For example, one of the permanent employees helped former First Lady Barbara Bush with a problem with her computer. It was a simple, innocent moment. But when Hillary heard about this, the employee was fired on the spot.
>
> In another case, a permanent staffer who worked in the White House residence objected to something Hillary wanted done with the furniture. Since the White House is a National Historic Site, there are rules and accountability for the furniture. This staffer's job involved enforcing those rules. But when she spoke up, she suddenly found herself the subject of an out-of-order FBI investigation, which is very similar to an IRS audit. Let me assure you, you do not want to be investigated by the FBI! But Hillary had no problem ordering such an investigation to punish this poor, innocent individual who was just trying to do her job.
>
> Then there was the way Hillary treated the Secret Service. She didn't seem to like these public servants who were there to protect her life. Say the Secret Service took a route she didn't like; she'd scream at them for it. Maybe they had a good reason, maybe not. But she had no sense of civility. . . .
>
> Then there was the time Hillary was considering how to move forward with her healthcare initiative. A group of business people wanted to meet her and talk about the ramifications of any changes in healthcare. She was forced to take the meeting because [she]

couldn't find a reason to say no. So these individuals from corporate America came to the White House and were forced to wait quite a while to talk to Hillary. Finally she marched through the door, threw their proposal on the table so that the pages scattered everywhere, swore at them in a loud voice, told them they had their blankety-blank meeting, and now she was finished with them, "Good day."

It is during these times that a person's true character comes out.

GREATEST FEAR OF HILLARY BACK IN THE WHITE HOUSE
Aldrich's greatest fear of Hillary, he says, "is her disrespect for the rule of law":

We are a nation of laws, and if powerful people disregard these laws, that creates a real danger to our individual liberties and freedoms.

This doesn't have anything to do with a woman in the White House. There are plenty of qualified women who are on their way up to a position of running for presidency. Let's look at those qualified women. And let's choose one that has genuine leadership capabilities.

For just a moment, let us interrupt the testimony of those who have worked directly for the Clintons. Mark Levin, the nationally renowned lawyer-turned-radio-host who once was the chief of staff for the U.S. attorney general, has similar views on Mrs. Clinton's ethics:

As a substantive matter, when you look at the things she has done in politics, she's always surrounded by sleaze and always doing things that seem to be sleazy, whether it is Castle Grande or Whitewater. Oh, she wasn't charged with anything. Well, you know she did go before a grand jury. I believe she lied in front of that grand jury.

She said she didn't know where her Rose Law Firm billing records were, and they pop up in the residence with her fingerprints on them, and maybe one or two other people's fingerprints on them. I don't know how they got there, but I have to assume she put them there.

And she's done other things that are extremely troubling: the way she hammered the Travel Office folks. These are just "little people" doing their jobs. She wanted them thrown in prison; she sicced the FBI on them.

The FBI files that were in the White House . . . They always have an answer. They always have an excuse.

The laundering of the Red China military money into their campaign: you know, this would bring down most politicians. But she is steeped in controversy, steeped in sleaze. That's why they don't want us to look at her record.

BUZZ PATTERSON

During the Clinton years, Lt. Col. Robert "Buzz" Patterson held one of the most important duties in the military. He was the president's senior military aide, responsible for carrying the "nuclear football." What he experienced drove him to write the *New York Times* best seller *Dereliction of Duty: The Eyewitness Account of How Bill Clinton Compromised America's National Security* (Regnery, 2004). Buzz Patterson's stories about the dangers both Bill and Hillary Clinton placed America into are at once harrowing and instructive for the electoral decisions voters now face:

I had been flying airplanes for the air force, stationed in northern California. I received a phone call to come in and meet with the president's military aide in Washington, D.C. There were several days of intense interviews.

They asked why I wanted the job, and I told them I didn't want the job, I was happy flying airplanes. I suppose that's what they wanted to hear. That evening I got a phone call from the White House saying, "We want you to be the military aide to the president of the United States."

As a major in the air force, you don't say no to that. This was November 1995. My first day in the White House was in April 1996. I remember walking in the White House on a beautiful spring day in Washington, D.C. The birds were chirping, the sun was shining, and I thought, *Here I am; I'm a major in the air force. I've arrived. I've got a White House bedroom and a White House office.* I was tickled to death, and thrilled to be President Bill Clinton's military aide.

I met the president and staff and got briefed by the Office of Special Programs on what to do if the president is shot at, where to evacuate him to, how to get him out of Washington, D.C. And so the first forty-eight hours was a blur.

The military aide actually dates back to George Washington. The position evolved with the Cold War during Presidents Eisenhower and Kennedy. The aide became the one tasked with carrying the Nuclear Football, which is a large black satchel [that] accompanies the president no matter where he is in the world, twenty-four hours a day. It's the means by which the president, as commander in chief, can always be in communication with the Pentagon in a crisis and, should it be necessary, launch nuclear weapons. So it's obviously an awesome responsibility.

As most people will tell you, Bill Clinton is very charismatic. He was bigger than I thought. Of course, his aura and his charisma preceded him. He looked me in the eye, shook my hand, welcomed me, and I recall thinking, *I just met the president!* My initial reaction was that he was a very nice guy, and I was just thrilled to be working with him.

Not so with the first lady.

In fact, in my briefings I recall my predecessor saying, "At some point in your two years here, you're going to make one of them mad; make sure it's not her." That was very good advice. When I first met Mrs. Clinton, she was very businesslike, very matter-of-fact. She didn't like to be around people in the White House.

I learned that the first lady didn't want to have to make eye contact with the people in the White House. Even senior staff members were not allowed to look her in the eye. It became very comical with grown adults diving into office doors to avoid her line of sight.

I know this sounds totally unbelievable, but others will tell you the same thing: apparently Hillary wanted to be able to move through the White House without all the usual "Good morning, good afternoon" exchanges. Ask any staffer during the Clinton years—we dove into doorways to avoid her wrath!

MORE INTERESTED IN WATCHING GOLF THAN KILLING BIN LADEN

Lt. Col. Patterson's enthusiasm for working the White House changed abruptly in December 1996:

I was attending a golf tournament with President Clinton. It was the President's Cup in Manassas, Virginia. Saddam Hussein had been annihilating the Kurds in northern Iraq, and on this day we were encouraging the Kurds to overthrow Hussein. The U.S. had pledged our support to the Kurds. We had fighters and bombers in the air over the Persian Gulf.

And on this day, I received three phone calls from Sandy Berger, the national security advisor, trying to get through to the president to launch an air attack in support of the Kurds. On all three occasions, I tried to hand the phone to the president—telling him it was urgent—and he waved me off. He wanted to watch golf.

What troubled me wasn't so much that the president wouldn't

say yes to the strike; it was that the president wouldn't even take the phone call. Because of his inability to focus on the mission at hand, the strike was canceled and thousands of Kurds [were] slaughtered.

As we drove back to the White House in the motorcade that day, I wondered, *Who have we elected as our commander in chief?*

Over the next two years, I was driven to the conclusion that Bill Clinton was unequipped to be our commander in chief. He never took military affairs realistically. He was more concerned about his own popularity in the polls. It was simply too risky for him to make a decision that involved the military because it might affect his poll popularity.

Time and again he would be given an opportunity to accept custody of bin Laden or to kill bin Laden, and he would choose not to because he was risk-adverse.

I think he was deeply affected by the deaths of the eighteen soldiers in the Black Hawk Down incident in Somalia. It happened early in his presidency. He saw how military affairs could be messy, how they could impact him adversely. So he resolved to use the military when it could help his political popularity, but not for the reason the military exists—to protect our interests. . . .

The biggest security breach during Clinton's term, perhaps the biggest security breach in our nation's history, was the time he actually lost the nuclear codes! . . .

One day I asked him to give me his set of codes, so I could give him a new set. Only then did he admit he lost them. My mind went racing a thousand directions. I didn't know how long the codes had been missing—hours, days, weeks?

How long had we not had the capability, should our nation be attacked, to respond? He didn't care. He was more concerned that the codes might fall into the hands of the media than all the other unspeakable possibilities. The guy's lack of focus was simply stunning.

I think it is relevant to mention that the president lost the nuclear codes on the day the Monica Lewinsky travesty hit the press. He was more distracted than I had ever seen him. His concern was that the nation was about to catch him with his pants down, literally. When you consider how badly national security could have been breached, you know just how risky the Clinton presidency really was.

CLEAR WARNINGS ABOUT TERRORISM, BUT NO ACTION

It is certainly easy to Monday-morning quarterback a president with the benefit of hindsight. It's not so easy when you're on the field, making decisions in real-time with only limited time and information on which to act. So is it fair to be critical of Bill Clinton's attempts to take out bin Laden? Here are the events of December 1996; you be the judge.

One of the documents that the president gets every day is called the Presidential Daily Briefing. PDB, for short. It's a compilation of intelligence reports from the FBI, CIA, Pentagon, and National Security Council. I was retrieving the PDB from President Clinton's desk, to take it back to the National Security Council.

Glancing at it, I keyed on one line in the report that talked about Operation Bojinka—the plot to use commercial airliners as weapons in the U.S., and about other plots to hijack airlines and fly them into the Pentagon, CIA headquarters, and New York City.

This was December 1996, and it was our first real insight into bin Laden. For the next two years, we tracked bin Laden and knew of the potential for terrorist attacks. Our nation had already been attacked by bin Laden on several occasions. Bin Laden became a fixture on President Clinton's radar screen. However, in the two years I was there, the president passed on several opportunities to take out bin Laden.

America was attacked eight times in the eight years of the

Clinton presidency. These were acts of war, publicly identified as such by bin Laden and others. Yet Clinton chose not to take any military action of consequence.

The one time he used military might to go after bin Laden was in the bombing of an aspirin factory in the Sudan. And at what point in time did he do that? It happened at the time Monica Lewinsky was up on Capitol Hill testifying against him in his impeachment trial.

A lot of people ask why we make so much of Clinton's dalliances. "When Clinton lied, nobody died" is the response liberals have. Well, when Clinton lied about his dalliances, bin Laden was ignored, and people died on 9/11, and they're still dying today.

Often these days on the campaign trail, Mrs. Clinton insists that if her husband had been warned about airlines being used as weapons, he would have done something. Fact is, the Clinton administration had ample opportunity and ample intelligence to take action, yet they did absolutely nothing. They are rewriting history. I think they have the O. J. Simpson inability to admit guilt for anything.

And in the coming years, an inability to face up to the facts of the international situation we're facing could be devastating. We're facing a global war against Islamic fascism. It's not just al-Qaeda, it's global Islamic Fascists—much like we faced against Nazism, fascism, and also communism. It's a global ideological struggle that's going to be with us for a long time.

Add in North Korea arming themselves with nuclear weapons. Iran arming themselves with nuclear weapons. China becoming an economic power, already with nuclear weapons. You're looking at a world much like 1939, 1940.

The Democrats and Mrs. Clinton have shown themselves to be quick to appease and to negotiate. They are like Neville Chamberlain trying to strike a bargain with Hitler. Today, like in the 1930s, we have an enemy that shows no interest in being appeased, no interest in negotiating. We need a commander in chief who can stand tall and strong.

COULD HILLARY COMMAND RESPECT FROM THE TROOPS?

It's essential in a military organization that you have leadership by example. And of course morale is very important to a military unit. The lowliest ranks in the military can see through somebody who lacks leadership in a heartbeat. They're very quick to remind those of us who have served as commanders when we're failing them as leaders—both in the example we set and in the morale we inspire.

I don't think Mrs. Clinton understands what it means to serve in the military, what it means to sacrifice.

In the Clintons we have people who are totally self-absorbed, driven by egos and the power they can attain. I don't think either of them wants to change and to actually learn about what makes our military so important at this critical time in history—and that is very troubling.

I look at how Mrs. Clinton took a position on the Senate Armed Services Committee, and I know she wants us to believe she's changed. I'd like to believe she's changed—since she's now a breath away from the Oval. But knowing Mrs. Clinton as I have known her, having served and lived with her for two years, I can see no possible way she's changed.

The war in Iraq and Afghanistan is the first real Internet war. Our soldiers can for the first time see what we're seeing, they can communicate with the States, and they can see what the media is reporting—all on a real-time basis.

They see when Mrs. Clinton says something stupid about the war; they see it played immediately on Al-Jazeera in the cafes and homes in Iraq. That does nothing to support the troops. All it does is embolden the enemy to believe that if they can hang on a little longer, they can win. And our troops, except for a few malcontents, know this!

The backlash from the military, if we are unfortunate enough to elect Hillary Clinton in 2008, will be significant. Most of the guys and gals over there, some of them in their second and third tours, are still riding on high morale. They know they're doing a good job. Sure, mistakes have been made. They know that. Mistakes are made in every war. But they know the importance of this war. And they don't want to lose this war in the States. They don't want to lose politically, which is what will happen if Hillary is elected. . . .

Much like her husband, Hillary Clinton's ideologies are based on a loathing of the military. I don't think she or her husband have ever understood what a military is for. I think you would see her use the military as a social Petri dish for everything from homosexual rights, to advancing radical feminism, to environmentally friendly issues. The military is not designed for that.

I don't see anything Hillary has done in the Senate that would lead me to believe otherwise. In fact, if anything, she has shown herself to be more committed to the ideology of the Left than her husband was. And that would be even more damaging to the military than her husband was.

Over his eight-year term, Bill Clinton hollowed out the military. Cutbacks in equipment and manpower. Deployments that were needless. He had inherited the fall of the Berlin Wall and the Iron Curtain, and he assumed this massive peace dividend. He thought that history was over; thought there would be no more conflict, no more world struggles, and he set about cutting 35 percent to 40 percent from the military budget.

At the same time, he deployed our forces a record forty times over eight years in what I call "CNN diplomacy." It wasn't to protect the U.S. national security interests abroad. It was to go into places like Haiti, Rwanda, Kosovo, Sierra Leon—places that would give him a bump in the polls at the expense of our military.

Bill Clinton put his personal desires first, creating vulnerability to blackmail. He was, and still is, a security risk. And Mrs. Clinton is ill-equipped to be commander in chief. If she wins, I think you'll see servicemen and -women voting with their feet. Many will just leave the service rather than serve under an unreliable commander in chief.

THE BIGGER CONCERN IS HER REMARKABLE TEMPER

What concerned me most in my day-to-day interactions with Mrs. Clinton was how quick she was to anger, how very vindictive and hard she could be on the people she depended on for day-to-day operations of the White House. It could be a quick, spontaneous fury. And it was very real. That's not the person you want with her finger on the nuclear button.

I saw her vent on her husband many times. Most vivid was the time we were going to a fund-raiser at a Washington, D.C., hotel. Mrs. Clinton had just learned that she was not going to be granted immunity from the Justice Department in the investigation of the Whitewater land deal. She was holding her husband responsible for this, for some reason. As we entered the elevator, she lit into him with every profane four-letter word you've ever heard in your life— and as a military guy, I've heard them all. The intensity of her anger really took me by surprise—how fast she could fly off the handle, how vicious she could be, how profane. Then, of course, the elevator door opened to the crowds and the two of them were holding hands and smiling and waving.

They could turn it on and off in a heartbeat. She was the quintessential actor, much like her husband.

EQUAL PARTNERS IN THE POLITICS OF DESTRUCTION

But whenever Bill got himself in trouble, as with Monica Lewinsky, Hillary took over and ran crisis-management meetings upstairs in the residence. In her biography, she says she didn't know about Monica until later that summer. It's important to understand that both Clintons are pathological liars. They will say or do anything to achieve the power they're looking for. For example, Mrs. Clinton made a big show of going onto the *Today Show* and claiming that the Monica Lewinsky accusations were the result of a "vast right-wing conspiracy."

I had been there. I knew of Monica Lewinsky. Most of the senior staff knew Monica Lewinsky. Secret Service agents knew of Monica Lewinsky. Mrs. Clinton knew of Monica Lewinsky. And we all knew long before the press got a hold of the story. In my first couple of days on the job, I realized that this intern had unusual access to the Oval Office, especially on weekends. Mrs. Clinton had her staff reassign Monica to the Pentagon—kind of suggests she knew what was going on, eh?

Mrs. Clinton knew all the potential skeletons in the closets. She was very involved in making sure that potential bimbo eruptions stayed as quiet as possible. In some ways, she was the puppeteer behind Bill—telling him what to say, how to act, what to do in certain situations. I was not privy to the meetings that were held in the residence immediately after the Monica story broke. But I do know that Mrs. Clinton attended all those meetings.

Author Ann Coulter has words to describe Hillary's attitude:

Mendacious, venal, sneaky. Sociopath-enabling. Liar is a good one; I believe you mentioned some others had raised that. Power mad.

But back to Lt. Col. Patterson, who had his eyes opened the hard way:

You know, I came from a family of Southern Democrats in North Carolina. But being a military officer for fifteen years, I was a political blank slate and would have been honored to serve any president and first lady. But when I walked out two years later, I was no longer a blank slate. So many recollections shed light on the real character of Mrs. Clinton.

Once we were helicoptering from the South Lawn to Andrews Air Force Base. We were halfway there. Suddenly Mrs. Clinton realized that she'd left her sunglasses back in the limousine. She demanded that the pilot turn Marine One around to go back to get her sunglasses.

To go back would have been foolish on so many levels, not the least of which would be the security breach—endangering her safety and the president's safety. We were finally able to convince her that it was not a good idea to go back. But she was beside herself screaming and ranting about going back!

On another occasion, we were on a family vacation flying from Hilton Head, South Carolina, to Saint Thomas and the Virgin Islands. Chelsea was along, and she had a backpack full of her college books. As we landed in Saint Thomas, Mrs. Clinton realized that Chelsea's backpack was still back in Hilton Head. Hillary went on a tear. It was everybody's fault, ironically, but Chelsea's. She demanded to know who had forgotten the books. She verbally thrashed her personal aide. She insisted that at taxpayer expense we launch Air Force One to go back to Hilton Head, grab the backpack, and bring it to Saint Thomas so Chelsea could study for her tests. In Hillary's mind, it couldn't possibly be Chelsea's fault, although she was a freshman at Stanford and could be expected to be a little responsible.

You know, I had not planned to go public about this. But I was so troubled by the misbehavior of the man we had entrusted as commander in chief. When he didn't support the Kurds in 1996, when he lost the nuclear codes in 1998, when he forfeited chance after chance to take out bin Laden, I had to speak out. I know we could have prevented 9/11. Bill Clinton let our country down like none before him. And I don't see Hillary Clinton being any different.

DICK MORRIS

Called "the most influential private citizen in America" by *Time*, Mr. Morris has known Bill and Hillary since 1977 and has directed a number of their campaigns. He has authored several books, including *Rewriting History* (HarperCollins, 2004), a refutation of Hillary's biography *Living History* (Simon & Schuster, 2003); and *Condi vs. Hillary* (HarperCollins, 2005). For those who have had enough of the old Clinton scandals, Dick Morris has uncovered new scandals Hillary will have to hurdle to win the presidency.

IS HILLARY GOING TO REVIVE HER CONTROVERSIAL IMMIGRATION PLAN?

Morris knows that a lot of people wonder how Hillary would handle the huge immigration problem we have. Well, he knows what she'd do:

> Because in 2004 she cosponsored a bill called the SOLVE Act, which stands for Safe Orderly Legal Visa Enforcement. Under this act, if an illegal immigrant were able to dodge the cops for five years and not get caught, he would automatically get on a track to citizenship, get health insurance for his children, and get in-state tuition at the state university.
>
> So when Hillary speaks of an "earned path to citizenship," she's not talking about learning English. She's talking about dodging the

cops for five years. Some way to earn it! I think that if Hillary is elected, the SOLVE Act is the one she'll go with.

HILLARY HAS ALREADY HINTED ABOUT HER PLANS FOR OUR TAXES

In Morris's opinion, the biggest change of a Hillary Clinton presidency would be the increase in taxes:

Get out your adding machine, and an aspirin too.

Right now the top tax bracket is 35 percent. She's going to raise it back up to 39.6 percent, which is where Bill raised it. She has said as much.

Secondly, she'll repeal the cut in the capital gains tax, taking it from 15 percent back up to 30 percent or even 35 percent. She's also said that.

The third thing she'll do, and it's something she doesn't talk about much, is raise Social Security taxes by eliminating or raising the threshold up to which you pay them. Right now you only pay Social Security taxes on the first $100,000 that you and your spouse make. Hillary will either raise or eliminate that ceiling. Let's say she raises it to $200,000. If you're self-employed and you and your spouse make $200,000, your taxes will double from $12,500 to $25,000.

So when you put it all together—a raise in the income tax rate, higher tax on capital gains, and a higher ceiling on Social Security taxes—if your family is making $200,000 a year you can count on coughing up $30,000 as the price of a Hillary Clinton presidency.

WILL SHE FINALLY DECIDE WE HAVE TO FIGHT TERRORISM AGGRESSIVELY?

Hillary will make us more vulnerable to terrorists because she will repeal the provisions of the Patriot Act. . . . Mohammed Babar is the guy who was planning to blow up half of downtown London. Would have killed hundreds if not thousands of people. Another 9/11. And how did we catch him?

He had gone into the New York Public Library and used the computer to communicate with his confederates in Pakistan and Afghanistan. Because of the Patriot Act, we could read what he was doing in the library, and we arrested him before he launched the operation. That disaster would not have been stopped if Hillary had her way.

Hillary has been most vocal in her opposition of wiretapping without a warrant by the National Security Agency (NSA). Again, let me give you an example of why it is vitally necessary that we give our security forces wiretapping capability. . . .

You see, the NSA does not routinely wiretap individual phones. Instead, they blanket wiretap millions of phone calls between Americans and people abroad. They don't know who to wiretap or what to look for. But they scan them all for anomalous phrases and things that seem out of the ordinary. One day they picked up the words "Brooklyn Bridge" being mentioned repeatedly. Apparently it doesn't translate well into Arabic.

Now in the old days, if NSA had a suspicion like this one, they couldn't have acted meaningfully. If they went to a judge and asked for a warrant for "anything that says Brooklyn Bridge," they would probably get nothing. Or if a warrant was granted, what could NSA do with it? Nothing.

But when the wiretaps picked up the words "Brooklyn Bridge" being said over and over, NSA alerted the New York City Police Department. Ray Kelly, NYPD commissioner, flooded the bridge with cops. So what happened next? NSA picked up a wiretap saying it was "too hot on the Brooklyn Bridge, too hot." The terrorists called off the attack. And what kind of an attack were they planning?

It turns out that soon after, we arrested the mastermind behind 9/11, and he confessed to the plot to blow up the bridge and named names. We raided the terrorist's apartment and found explosives, plus a diagram of where to place the bomb to bring the bridge down.

Now if Hillary had had her way, there would have been no wire-tap intercept, no interrogation of the 9/11 mastermind without his attorney, and no Brooklyn Bridge—it would be in the East River.

WITH HILLARY, YOU HAVE TO READ BETWEEN THE LINES ON IRAQ

"As a public service," says Dick Morris, "here's a clarification of Hillary's position on Iraq":

Hillary said we should have gone into Iraq, and she voted for the war resolution. Then after she found out there were no weapons of mass destruction, she said it was worthwhile going in anyway because we had to get rid of Saddam Hussein. Then she said it was a mistake to be in Iraq the way we were doing it, but that she was still right to vote in favor of sending us in originally. But she said she'd never vote to withdraw our troops, she'd never vote for a deadline, and she'd never vote to cut off funding while troops are in harm's way. Then seven months later she voted to withdraw the troops, set a deadline, and cut off funding. So that's her position on Iraq. Everyone clear?

HILLARY IS THE CLOSEST THING WE HAVE TO A EUROPEAN SOCIALIST

Hillary deeply believes that that government should vastly expand its efforts in the areas of healthcare, education, nutrition, and children.

She believes government should not take 33 percent of our income in taxes; it should take more like the midforties or high-forties like France and Germany and many Scandinavian countries do. . . .

She believes that those who oppose her programs to expand government are truly evil people. And as a result, she believes that the ends fully justify the means and that she can do anything to achieve political power—because her ends are so worthwhile.

From an outsider's vantage point, author Ann Coulter adds some insight to that:

When the candidates were asked about education . . . Hillary said, because education begins in the family, she would send social workers, visiting nurses, to every family that has just had a newborn baby. She wants to send government workers to your house because you've had a baby. That's Hillary Clinton's plan. Did you see that in any headline? I think that is kind of newsworthy. This is like Winston Smith in [the novel] *1984*. Big Brother is going to be there every moment of every day. That's part of her to-do list.

WHY I PARTED COMPANY WITH HILLARY CLINTON

Dick Morris finally parted company with Hillary Clinton when he

saw how she used private detectives to snoop on the women her husband was involved with. Not to reform him, not to divorce him, not to change him, but to cow the women into silence about her husband. I do not want that woman controlling the IRS or the DEA or the NSA or the FBI or the CIA. Not in a democracy, I don't.

HILLARY WANTS TO BE JUDGED ON HER EXPERIENCE. OKAY . . .

Her experience is supposed to be the big difference between her and Barack Obama. She has it, and he doesn't. Well, what experience? When Hillary's husband was first elected president, she was given charge of healthcare reform. She messed it up beyond all recognition during '93 and '94. She was essentially out of the White House in '95, '96, and '97. I know, because I was there most of that time. She was running around the world, visiting seventy countries, writing a best-selling book, doing book signings.

Then she came back during the Lewinsky scandal in '98 and her job was damage control—to keep her husband in office. Then in '99 and 2000 she spent her time running for the Senate.

In the Senate, she's passed very, very little. Her voting record is an incredibly liberal one. She has in no way made a significant imprint there. All she really did was raise a lot of money for Democrats and write another best-selling book, making $8 million for it. So where is this experience?

IF OUR PRESIDENT THINKS SHE'S ABOVE THE LAW, WHO LOSES?

Hillary should have learned her lesson in 1996 when the Clintons were publicly embarrassed for raising money from people who spent the night in the Lincoln bedroom. But in her Senate campaign of 2000, of the 404 people who were invited to sleep in the White House, 146 gave money to the Democratic Party, and 100 gave money to Hillary Clinton. She didn't learn a thing.

[As detailed in chapter 1,] Hillary had a Hollywood producer named Peter Paul throw a big fund-raiser for her. The fund-raiser brought in a lot of contributions, but the problem was that it cost over a million dollars to stage. So she had her campaign staff claim that the fund-raiser cost only $300,000 or so, not the million plus it really was. That gave her an additional $700,000 in hard cash to spend on the Senate campaign. Her campaign was fined $35,000 by the Federal Elections Commission—it amounted to one of the biggest frauds in FEC history.

HILLARY IS IN BED WITH BILL, WHO IS IN BED WITH UNSCRUPULOUS OPERATORS

Bill and Hillary Clinton share finances. So what Bill earns, Hillary earns. It goes into their joint checking account. There is a company named infoUSA that unscrupulously sells telemarketing lists to shady operators who, as detailed in the *New York Times*, use these lists to fleece the elderly. Some of the lists they sell have titles such as *Elderly with Alzheimers* and *Gullible Seniors* and *People Over 55 Who Think Their Luck Will Change.* These are infoUSA's own titles for their lists!

InfoUSA has paid Bill Clinton, and therefore Hillary Clinton, $3.3 million in direct income since Hillary has been senator. InfoUSA has also paid $900,000 for vacations for the Clintons, plus $1 million for the Clinton library, plus $2 million for a New Year's celebration for Hillary. Hillary and Bill Clinton should not be in hock to people of this ilk.

And Hillary has never answered the key question: What did infoUSA get for all that money they paid the Clintons, or what will they get? And did the payments made to the Clintons help infoUSA rip off these poor elderly people?

HOW HILLARY COLDLY AND CYNICALLY "PLAYED" THE TRAGEDY OF 9/11

After 9/11, Hillary had a problem. She was the senator from New York, and yet her connection with the state was very, very limited. The state needed a senator who understood New York, not an import from Arkansas. A lot of the cops and firemen and rescue workers were really down on her. In fact, they booed her at a rally in Madison Square Garden. So Hillary tried to create a connection between the 9/11 tragedy and herself.

She went on the *Today Show* and claimed Chelsea had been in harm's way on 9/11, that she had been jogging around the World Trade Center and was saved only because she ducked into a coffee shop at the last minute.

Well, Chelsea later gave an interview to *Talk Magazine* saying that she was actually at a friend's apartment four or five miles away, and she saw the whole thing over television when a friend woke her up. She had been asleep in bed!

Hillary surely knew as much long before she went on the *Today Show*. Somebody capable of that low a fabrication on national television should not be president.

A WOMAN FOR PRESIDENT OF THE UNITED STATES?

Should a woman be elected president of the United States? Yes. Is America ready for a woman president? You bet. But not Hillary Clinton. There are three reasons not to vote for her:

First, she's very liberal. Huge increase in taxes, huge increase in the public sector if she's elected president.

Second, she's vengeful with a long list of enemies, a long list of people to get even with. You don't want her controlling the IRS and the FBI and all the agencies that can needle into our lives.

Third, she's deceitful. She'll make up any story or lie about anything, as long as it serves her purpose. You're looking at four years of not being able to believe what your president says.

| 9 |

DO WOMEN WANT *THIS* WOMAN IN THE WHITE HOUSE?

The 2008 election could be a historic first with a woman becoming president for the first time in our nation's history. Hillary herself is certainly aware of history's anticipation. And from the outset of her campaign, she has sought in subtle ways to make this an election about women. Not *a* woman, but *women.*

So in addition to the general commentary that we elicited from our interviewees, we asked our female commentators to focus additionally on Hillary from the perspective solely of women. Four of our film's (and book's) participants rose to the challenge:

• BAY BUCHANAN
Author of *The Extreme Makeover of Hillary (Rodham) Clinton* (Regnery, 2007) and former treasurer of the United States, appointed by Reagan.

• AMANDA CARPENTER
Reporter with *Townhall.com* and author of *The Vast Right-Wing Conspiracy's Dossier on Hillary Clinton* (Regnery, 2006).

• KATE O'BEIRNE

Washington editor for *National Review* and author of *Women Who Make the World Worse: And How Their Radical Feminist Assault Is Ruining Our Schools, Families, Military, and Sports* (Sentinel, 2006).

• ANGELA MCGLOWAN

Author of *Bamboozled: How Americans Are Being Exploited by the Lies of the Liberal Agenda* (Nelson, 2007), she understands how Hillary Clinton tries to bamboozle minorities.

WHY DO SO MANY WOMEN DEFEND AND LIE FOR THE CLINTONS?

Power. It's a word that came up time and again in our interviews. The left-wing leaders of the Democratic Party put up with Bill and Hillary, says Kate O'Beirne, for one reason:

> It is about power and clout, not about the well-being of women.
>
> They cover for him in his mistreatment of women because he has defended abortion rights, comparable worth, and day care. That is the bargain they have struck. He supported a left-wing feminist agenda, so his mistreatment of women is supposed to be irrelevant. That is the message they send to younger women.
>
> Hillary Clinton has been publicly humiliated by an abusive husband, she has even enabled this abusive behavior, and yet she is held up as this paragon of feminist virtue. That she is reveals the hypocrisy of the modern women's movement.

Hillary's quest for power goes back fifty years, notes Bay Buchanan:

> In her high school yearbook, Hillary commented that she would like to be married to a senator. So, very early in life she saw that power

would be something that would interest her. But at that time, she saw herself one step behind the power, giving her access to power. She married the man who told her he was going to [be] president someday. So she did everything possible to get him there. Once he got there, they had a copresidency, and she was able to enjoy an incredible feeling of power as first lady. Once she had tasted that power, it was her turn.

So many of the Clintons' supporters were simply complicit in wanting power, but others, Angela McGlowan tells us, were conned:

The Clintons are bamboozlers. Ronald Reagan said, "Don't be afraid to see what you see." Malcolm X said, "You been had, you been took, you been hoodwinked, you been bamboozled." Well, Hillary Clinton gave a speech in a black church in Selma, Alabama. And she borrowed James Cleveland's famous hymn, "I don't feel no ways tired . . ." Now some people say that she was just using a Southern accent, harmless enough. No.

She was using a black dialect to fit in with black folk when her world couldn't be further away. That's what the Clintons are infamous for. They make these symbolic gestures and don't do a dadgum thing about creating a better America for black people. That's bamboozling!

Now there's nothing wrong with a politician trying to relate to her audience, if it results in genuine action for that audience. But in the Clintons' case, what action are we talking about? The action of Bill Clinton in 2001 receiving the first Black President Award from the Congressional Black Caucus—so everyone can pretend he's black? Or the action of Bill Clinton setting up his postpresidency office in Harlem—I'll bet he's been there maybe three times. These are not real actions. This is pulling the wool over. This is bamboozling!

WILL THE ELECTION TURN ON THE SINGLE WHITE FEMALE VOTE?

From the beginning of the campaign, pollsters have been telling us that the 2008 presidential election could turn on the "single white female" vote. We asked Amanda Carpenter, who falls into this demographic, what she would advise a woman who was thinking of voting for Hillary Clinton:

> I would ask the woman if she thinks she can trust Hillary Clinton. As a reporter assigned to Capitol Hill, I see her walking around with her staff, her secret service, and no reporter can penetrate. She only talks to reporters when we pigeonhole her, or when she has a script. The women I know and like in my life tend to be warm, inviting, talkative, friendly. Can't say that about Hillary.
>
> There was one time I saw her beneath the Senate floor at a luncheon with partisans, and she was being friendly. She really was. She smiled; she acted like a normal person. But as soon as she walked out of that door and saw someone like me with a microphone, the smile was gone. And I wondered why? Why doesn't she want to talk to reporters unscripted? Best I can ascertain, it's because she can't trust herself not to be herself—which always gets her in trouble. And that is where I would start with someone who doesn't know Hillary. I would ask, "How do you trust your vote to someone who can't be herself, who can't be honest in public?"
>
> I recall the first time I interviewed Hillary Clinton, I was an intern doing a benign piece called "Books Politicians Are Reading." We were just two young girls, smiling, excited to be in the Capitol. And my partner asked Hillary, "What is your favorite book?" Hillary turned away, saying, "I cannot answer that right now." But I kept after her, "What are you reading that is interesting?" This time Hillary said, "Call me at the office, and we will get back to you." What's the importance of this little story?

That Hillary won't do anything unless scripted. I mean, several senators at least said, "I'm reading the Bible," just to say something. She couldn't even do that.

As a reporter, I know that if you ask Hillary a question, she has only three possible responses. The first is, "Call my office," the second is, "I do not know," and the third is, "My staff will get back to you."

The 2008 election will turn *not only* on the single white female vote, says Angela McGlowan, but also on two other important constituencies:

There are three constituencies that are going to change the face of politics and decide our next president in 2008—that's women, blacks, and Latinos. Both political parties are reaching out to Latinos and talking about the immigration issue. I've interviewed many Latinos on the issue. What do they really want? What are they looking for in a leader?

Well, 77 percent of Latinos want English as the national language. But Hillary doesn't want to tackle that issue. Latinos do want people to come here legally—not to swim the river, or hop over a fence and then live in the shadows—but to come legally and not just pick fruit, but enjoy the fruits of the American dream. Latinos care about the economy and about access to capital—these are the real issues, the ones Hillary doesn't want to tackle.

I have a message for my black brothers and sisters: it's important to get out and vote. Not our color, not our culture, but our conscience. Too many black people just vote the Democratic ticket because we've been bamboozled into thinking that's what we're supposed to do!

IF ELECTED, WOULD HILLARY HAVE A "WOMEN'S AGENDA"?

If Hillary Clinton is elected president, it will be, according to Kate O'Beirne, a major victory for radical feminists:

Hillary could be expected to enthusiastically support the radical feminist agenda: the continued feminization of our classrooms; the kind of quotas on college campuses that have seen so many men's sports teams eliminated; newfangled regulations to solve a perceived wage gap between men and women . . .

When asked to write a short TV spot to educate female voters about Hillary, O'Beirne suggested these words:

The radical feminists believe there are no differences between men and women. They believe children do not need mothers and fathers. They believe social engineering ought to take place in the military. They believe young male athletes ought to face a quota on college campuses. They believe our classrooms ought to be feminized so little boys will behave more like little girls. If you believe in these things as well, vote for Hillary Clinton!

The biggest beneficiaries of a Hillary presidency could be government employees. Bay Buchanan expects Hillary to keep government employees very busy:

Right now Hillary is not really thinking about *What will I do as president?* as much as *I need to become president, so I'll have the power.* Within that context, she talks about the purpose of government being to remold society for the common good. She expects government to become extremely involved in the lives of the people in this country—because government knows best.

Her economic course would bring bigger government and higher taxes because she believes that the expertise of government is the best guide for our lives. She has said, "We cannot rely on people to make the right choices; government has to make the right choices." She has also said, "We need to tell parents how to raise children." She completely discounts the notion that parents might know what's in the best interest of their own children.

The historic importance of this election, in the view of Angela McGlowan, extends well beyond gender politics:

> Yes, with Hillary in the race this is a historic election for women. But you could say the same for Barack Obama—the first serious black contender for president. Or Mitt Romney—the first serious Mormon contender. Or Bill Richardson—the first serious Hispanic contender.
>
> This is in fact a wonderfully historic election that showcases all of the ethnicities and genders that form and shape the American twenty-first century. But personally, I want the most qualified candidate. Who will wage this war on terror? Who will improve education? If it's a woman or a black, so be it. But what's the logic in voting for somebody just because they look like you?

Kate O'Beirne also sees Hillary having to pretend to be something she is not:

> Hillary is far more liberal than she wants us to think. So she has to be very controlled. She cannot be too spontaneous. I think that is going to be a problem for her. It is inauthentic, and people can spot that. People begin wondering why she is not more comfortable being who she is.
>
> Bill Clinton was extremely fortunate because he is utterly comfortable in his own skin. Somebody else might not be that comfortable in Bill Clinton's skin, but he is comfortable there. Hillary Clinton does not have the same asset. For reasons I do not pretend to understand, she is not comfortable being herself. So she is trying to be someone else.

The mainstream media has been quick to relay Hillary's campaign assertion that she is a moderate candidate. Kate O'Beirne begs to differ:

> The reassuringly moderate portrayal of Hillary Clinton is directly contradicted by her voting record in the Senate. Her lifetime voting record is to the left of Teddy Kennedy. Her ACLU rating is higher than Barbara Boxer's—the liberal of California. She is on record as the second biggest spender in the Senate. She is going to have to defend a liberal voting record that's very much at odds with the moderate makeover.

IS HILLARY THE MODEL OF A MODERN MAJOR FEMINIST?

Hillary has long been something of an icon of her generation—the first student to speak at a Wellesley graduation, one of a small number of women at Yale Law School, a woman on the Nixon impeachment team, a first lady with a portfolio, and now a serious bid for the White House.

Along the way she has raised a daughter—apparently doing a fine job of it. And she has taken activist stands on the treatment of children—both in reaching out to children in genuine need and in increasing government involvement in the raising of children. So is Hillary a model for women? Angela McGlowan suggests that she's a walking, talking contradiction:

> Example: During the Imus scandal when he said those nasty words about the Rutgers athletes, Hillary went to Rutgers and talked about how awful the whole thing was. Okay, agreed. Then why did Hillary then accept $800,000 from a fellow named Timothy Z. Mosley at a fund-raiser in Los Angeles?
>
> Mosley, better known by his stage name Timbaland, is a big producer of songs riddled with the n-word, the b-word, and the h-word.

On several TV shows I challenged Hillary to give back the money, but of course she didn't. If she really cared, would she take $800,000 from someone who degrades women and glorifies violence?

And if she's taking big money from misogynists like Timbaland, what does she owe them?

Would she make Timbaland chairman of the Federal Communications Commission, where the broadcast standards would be amended to include the n-word, the b-word, and the h-word during family TV viewing hours? . . .

What upsets me most is how Hillary uses Al Sharpton and Jesse Jackson—biggest bamboozlers of all. These men are race baiters, using scare tactics and smear-and-fear campaigns to build up nothing more than their own oversized egos and bank accounts. What have they really done for black people?

Sharpton and Jackson are looking out for number one, period. If Hillary is keeping company with these bamboozlers, I keep in mind my mama's words: you are who you associate with.

Black America is in a state of crisis. Seven out of ten black babies are born out of wedlock. A lot of us are dropping out of school. A lot of us are not finding great jobs. And yet 90 percent of us give our vote to the Democratic Party because we're getting bamboozled by folks like Hillary.

We have several generations raised on hopelessness and despair, all the while being told by bamboozlers that more government programs are the solution. And what have those programs actually solved? Things have gone from bad to worse.

| 10 |

DOES ANYBODY *REALLY*
KNOW THIS WOMAN?

Over the last fifteen years, scores of voters, scholars, reporters, lawyers, and investigators alike have tried in one way or another to solve the mystery of Hillary Rodham Clinton. Who is she really? Will we ever know?

Of all the people who know the "private Hillary" and who would speak to us, few know her better than Michael Medved:

> I knew Hillary at Yale Law School. I went on a leave of absence after my first semester, but I continued to live by campus and socialize with law students. I had joined a senatorial campaign, which Hillary Rodham urged me to do. Hillary was certainly one of my best friends. She was terrific. . . .
>
> It was a strange environment. When you look at that class today—one is an IRS commissioner; one's a Supreme Court justice; one's a superagent in Hollywood. So it was very competitive, very intense. But Hillary was beyond that. There were no sharp elbows. She was not going to step on you to get ahead. There was a feeling of friendship, comradeship, kindness, and caring.
>
> Hillary was everybody's den mother. She was one of very few

women in the class of '72 at Yale Law who wasn't date bait. She didn't want to be. She was heavier; she wore sweatshirts and sandals and big black flowing pants. She was somewhat famous because of that speech she gave at Wellesley. They published the speech in *Life*, and I remember reading it, and saying, "This is awful; this doesn't make any sense at all." It was all about more ecstatic modes of being and all this woo-woo stuff. But it was all terribly sincere, and that was also part of Hillary.

She sincerely wanted to do good in the world and to live as a nice person. But something happened, obviously. A lot of people think the Hillary story is scary; I think it's terribly sad.

Hillary may not be as good a liar or an actor as her husband, but Congressman Dan Burton suggests that she had a master for a teacher:

Bill Clinton would have been a first-rate movie star. He could look right in the camera and tell the American people one thing, when he knew it was a lie. He was so good, people bought it. Even people in his own administration bought it. I remember when Ron Brown was killed in a plane crash, and Bill Clinton came out; he was laughing, telling a joke to somebody, and the minute he saw the TV camera he went, "Oh my God," and instantly teared up.

When you look at Hillary in action, you are struck by an apparent dichotomy: here is a woman who was capable of memorizing 1,300 pages of healthcare legislation, but who could not for two years find her Rose Law Firm billing records that were sitting there in the White House all along.

Bob Novak gets to the middle of the issue:

Senator Clinton has a talent for obfuscation, for sidestepping questions, for avoiding confrontations. And it has worked for her on one level, so she continues to do it. Think about it, she was very close to being prosecuted for her role in [the] Whitewater case, but her prevarications saved her. And, ironically, Monica saved her. When Special Prosecutor Ken Starr stumbled into the Lewinsky fiasco, it was a blessing for Hillary. It diverted the prosecutors from their focus on Hillary's transgressions—which very nearly resulted in the first-ever criminal prosecution of a first lady. So she has learned how to sidestep trouble very well.

American Spectator founder R. Emmett Tyrrell, who long has been a Clinton nemesis because his magazine uncovers so many of their scandals, thinks he has Hillary Clinton's psychology figured out:

We know Hillary is an insecure person. Secure people don't lie. They don't lie inveterately the way she does. . . . My suspicion is that insecurity somehow comes from her self-regard, her self-absorption, her narcissism—and narcissistic people, oddly enough, become very insecure when challenged. . . .

It's a recklessness that is born of an arrogance that does date back to her 1960s roots and their narcissism. They believe they are a rule unto themselves. [But] every time Hillary's been caught in a scandal, she *really* did it. No one made it up.

Talk show host Mark Levin picks up on these ideas:

The reason authenticity is difficult for Hillary Clinton is because if you strip away her makeup and her pants suit, what you will have is somebody who is so hard left and so radical—she has never changed—that the American people would be repulsed. The American people have never elected anybody as left wing and radical as Hillary Clinton. That's why they are trying to remake her into a centrist.

It seems that there is little in Hillary's past that has not been shredded, sliced up with scissors, lost in a closet then suddenly found, or redacted. Bob Novak suggests that things are going to change though:

It's true, we know little about how Hillary Clinton has operated. There is an enormous amount of material about her that is probably never going to be released.

But we're in a new political cycle now, a new day in which everybody's going to be looking at her more closely. She's not first lady now; she is not merely a senate candidate now; she is a presidential candidate now. I think there will be a more aggressive attitude by the media to dig into the truth of her many missteps.

Those Clinton years were chaotic in a dangerous way, former FBI agent Gary Aldrich warns, and we could expect the same group of people to return to the White House:

Many of the same people would return for round two. And I don't think they learned anything in round one. I've never heard an apology. I've never heard a reasonable explanation for their misconduct. I've never heard one of them say, "This was a growth experience." They came into the White House very arrogant, lacking in humility. They were unlike anyone I had ever seen serve in government.

If Hillary wins, it would suggest that Congressman Dan Burton would be back working around the clock:

I was chairman of the committee that investigated the White House for five years. We sent five criminal referrals to Janet Reno, head of the Justice Department. There was no question in my mind, or in the minds of the majority on the committee, that those were indictable offenses. Janet Reno was the best blocker I've ever seen. She would have been an All-Star in the NFL. Whatever we sent to her that might have caused heartburn to the Clinton administration, she blocked.

Some people try to cover for the Clintons by saying, "Okay, there were problems, but there were no indictments handed down." It's true, there were no indictments, but that doesn't mean there were no indictable offenses. There were. It's just that Janet Reno was such a good blocker.

If you thought there was corruption in the Bill Clinton White House, you can expect the same kind of activity in a Hillary Clinton White House. She'll do whatever's necessary—legal or illegal—to achieve her political ends.

On that investigative committee was also Congressman John Mica:

In investigating the Clintons, our main problem was just keeping up—it was scandal du jour. Every week there was some new revelation, one more stunning than the other. You hear the term *sticker shock*, this was "scandal shock," and people became numb to it. Do we really want a president that we become numb to?

I can tell you for a fact that the Clinton administration did mislead Congress; did lie to the Congress of the United States; did keep issues from ever becoming public because it would have hurt them badly.

Few will argue that the Clintons made mistakes in office—every administration makes mistakes. It is how one deals with one's mistakes, says Jeff Gerth, that defines a leader:

Whenever Hillary made a mistake, she would cover it up and end up compounding it. Back in 1992, for example, she was doing legal work for an S&L that, coincidentally, was in trouble with Arkansas State regulators. Bill was governor. There were obvious conflicts of interest. It turns out that during the campaign, she assembled a statement in which she acknowledged that she shouldn't have worked on the S&L case, because it didn't look right. But this statement was never released to the media.

So instead of admitting that she made a mistake, she hid it and actually lied in the course of the campaign about her work before her husband's regulators. As a result, she got locked into false statements and wound up having to testify under oath about those statements— leading to perjury. There were people in the independent counsel's office who thought her statements amounted to crimes. Others thought there wasn't enough evidence to go forward. And of course she was not charged, but she got as close as you can get to an indictment.

IS HILLARY CLINTON A LIBERAL, MODERATE, PROGRESSIVE, WHAT?

Hillary has held so many political positions over the years that pinning her down with a label or an ideology is difficult. Of all the questions our film and book participants addressed, this is the one that inspired the greatest range of opinions. For example, Bob Novak believes that Hillary will be whatever Hillary needs to be to succeed:

The next step for her is the presidency. Does that mean she should act like a moderate? It's not so clear.

Edward Klein agrees that Hillary could not have changed that much:

Hillary the president would be far different from Hillary the candidate. She is positioning herself as a moderate, as a centrist, as somebody who is experienced in foreign affairs and pro-military. This is all make-believe. This is not the Hillary that we have known and watched for thirty years. She can't possibly have changed her stripes that much.

When you're in the White House, you have to call upon your experiences. You never have the time for anything else. And I think Hillary will revert to her left-wing past.

Dick Armey combines the notions that Hillary is both a leftist and an opportunist:

First of all, understand that she is a very skilled and able politician. But also understand that politicians will say insincere things if they believe it will get your vote. Hillary Clinton pretends to stand in the middle of the road. But there is no way of judging her future except by her past as an antimilitary, proabortionist, big-governmenteer! That's who she is, though she pretends not.

As well, she has no deep religious faith that would make sense [to] the average American. She had a big infatuation a few years ago with communitarianism, which basically says the community is more important than the individual, equality is more important than opportunity. So that's what guided her, and it is consistent with the policy positions she has taken. Now you can say to me, "Who am I to pass judgment on her faith?"

And you're right; I am not making a judgment. I'm sure her faith, whatever it is, is as deeply held as mine. The rub here is that it's all pretenses. At the end of the day, she's a person who believes in big government. She will tax you to the hilt. She will redistribute your wealth. She will try to achieve equality of outcomes. She's a Big Government Liberal.

Hillary thinks government must intercede in your life, because either you are too incompetent to manage your own affairs and there-fore need the protection of the government, or you are too corrupt and therefore need the regulation of the government. Or maybe both. In any event, what you need to make her comfortable is more government in your life.

Now I have a lot of liberal friends, such as Congressman Ron Dellums. He's a left-winger who stands up and says it proudly, as he should. He doesn't pretend to be what he's not. If people are buying what you're selling, sell it honestly. If you want to be a left-winger, then go out and say so.

Mark Levin, radio talk show host and former top official at the Justice Department, says he knows exactly what to expect if Senator Clinton becomes president:

Hillary Clinton as president scares the hell out of me, and I'll tell you why. Her values are not the values of most Americans. And by that I mean she believes in an economic system that is contrary to our eco-nomic system. She is hostile to the military: she was when she was first lady; she's always been.

She will appoint the most radical activist judges ever in American history. She has made statements that are really totalitarian in nature, and I don't overstate it, about taking money from the oil companies, about undercapitalized small business; these are very radical statements.

Hillary is a 1960s radical retread, and they are trying to dress her up as a centrist so as not to scare the American people. But that is why people are backing her for president, not based on experience, because she has no presidential experience, or no experience that would lend itself to the presidency. [Her strategists] want her in office because she is a radical, and she will pursue radical policies. So that scares the hell out of me.

Whatever Hillary's real stripes, Bob Novak tells us that she is definitely not to be underestimated:

> Just as in 1980, a lot of Democrats underestimated Ronald Reagan; a lot of Republicans today think that because Hillary is unlikable, she's the candidate that'll be easiest to beat. But she is smart.
>
> Recall how in the first major debate the Democratic candidates were asked, "What would you do if American cities were attacked?"
>
> Senator Obama, the rookie, said some nonsense about first responders and warning systems—not a good answer.
>
> Hillary stepped up and knocked the question out of the park, saying that if the U.S. was attacked, she would retaliate.
>
> Whether she would or not, I don't know. But that was a great answer. So her adversaries in the Republican Party should not be deluded into thinking she's going to be easy to beat.

"JUDGE ME ON MY EXPERIENCE," SHE SAYS. OKAY.

Hillary is telling Americans that she is the "most experienced" candidate in the race and that she deserves credit for the successes of the Clinton administration. Theirs was touted as a copresidency, but is Hillary making an honest and accurate claim? As is her custom, Angela McGlowan cuts to the quick:

> Just because you're sleeping with the president, it doesn't mean you know how to run the country. If I'm sleeping with a firefighter, does that mean I know how to fight fires? What gives?

Tony Blankley thinks Hillary is misleading the public in two ways:

> First, it's worth noting that after her healthcare fiasco, the Clinton

team sidelined her. Gave her ceremonial duties only. She was more like a Pat Nixon than Eleanor Roosevelt from mid-1994 onward, because Bill Clinton's professionals recognized she made a hash of the one big policy initiative she'd been given. So for her to take credit for anything that happened after 1994 is hugely misleading.

Second, it was the Republican Congress that took the lead in the budget cutting, the tax cutting, and the welfare reform. Bill Clinton took credit for and bragged about how these initiatives gave rise to a strong economy. But they were largely the product of a Republican Congress that Hillary's husband signed onto.

As for having direct hands-on experience, Hillary has never managed anything more than a senate office. Her only other professional job was briefly as a lawyer when her husband was governor, and many of her clients wanted to get to know her husband better and hired her for that purpose. That's good qualifications for being a lawyer; whether that's good qualifications for being a president is another matter.

She makes it sound like she has diplomatic experience, like she has managerial experience, like she has policy development experience. She doesn't have any of those things, and the media has largely bought into her campaign claim that she's Miss Experience. She's far from it.

WHICH POLITICIAN IS HILLARY MOST SIMILAR TO?

Given Hillary's penchant for paranoia and prevarication, there's little surprise who she is often compared to and what that might mean for the conduct of the executive branch under her reign. Most interesting is the comparison made by Tony Blankley:

For about a year I've been using the phrase Hillary Milhous Clinton. I use it to be perhaps a little amusing, but also to make a fundamental point: there are real similarities between Hillary Clinton and Richard Nixon. Some complimentary, some not.

They're both highly intelligent; they're both ruthless; they both have great work habits; they're both cynical politically. It is ironic, of course, that she was part of the prosecuting team against Nixon when he was being threatened with impeachment by Congress, and now she has become the object of her former efforts. She has become the object she once hunted—the Moby Dick of the Left.

Hillary may succeed, as Nixon did, in getting elected. But the infirmities that brought Nixon down hang around Hillary, as well.

Edward Klein confirms another similarity between Nixon and Hillary:

Hillary thought herself, well, imperial. Early on Hillary's chief of staff Maggie Williams put out an order to all White House staffers telling them, "When you see Hillary, do not look her in the eye." It was as if she were Empress of Japan. You were supposed to avert your gaze for fear you might in some way upset "Empress Hillary."

Dick Morris takes the comparison a step further:

The president that Hillary reminds me of most is Richard Nixon. Hillary and Nixon have the same chip on their shoulder: the same belief that they're surrounded by enemies; the same belief that they have to get even; the same commitment to be deceitful when it serves their purpose; the same willingness to lie to the American people and try to fool them; the same ruthlessness in using all of the tools available—private detectives or the FBI or the CIA to try to break into people's homes and do negative things to them. All of that ruthlessness is really Nixonian.

Author Ann Coulter, unprompted, used identical terminology to describe Mrs. Clinton:

Absolutely ruthless!

Congressman Dan Burton disagrees:

I would not compare Hillary Clinton to Nixon. Watergate was a break-in; he shouldn't have authorized it; he was punished for it. The Clinton White House was far worse than Watergate. The Clintons were taking illegal campaign contributions from the Chinese communist government, according to Johnny Chung, who testified before our committee.

The pattern is a familiar one. Huge amounts of money are raised, and questions follow. Last summer Mrs. Clinton was forced to return nearly $900,000 from fugitive Norman Hsu, who is now under investigation for running a Ponzi scheme. This echoes the shenanigans during the White House years, when it was the dirty money of Charlie Trie and Johnny Chung—both convicted of illegal campaign fund-raising.

Congressman Dan Burton continues:

It was Johnny Chung . . . that said, "The White House was like a subway turnstile: You put the money in, and you got in."

Columnist and author John Fund picks up on that image:

And his tokens were very large of course. There's evidence that he collected money from a Chinese intelligence officer . . . trying to influence our elections to gain access to decision-making powers in the

United States so they would bend U.S. policy toward China. . . . The campaign finance scandals were so extensive, 120 people either fled the country to avoid being interrogated by investigators, pleaded the Fifth Amendment, or otherwise avoided questions. Fourteen guilty pleas came out of that.

Author and columnist Michael Barone talks about how obviously fishy the 2007 case was, right from the start:

The *Los Angeles Times* story on the Clinton campaign contributions from dishwashers in Chinatown. . . . I'm a little surprised that some-one in the campaign didn't flag that down and say, "Dishwashers?!— Maximum contributions, or thousands of dollars? Let's look into that a little bit." The *Los Angeles Times* looked into that and found they couldn't find something like a third of these contributors, and they found others who said they had no idea that they had made these contributions. It looks like a clear case that somebody committed campaign fund-raising law violations and that the Clinton campaign did not do due diligence to track that down.

Jeff Gerth has written less than kindly about a "twenty-year project" that the Clintons have. The obvious question about such a plan is, what's so wrong with having a dream or an ambition?

Yes, what is wrong with being ambitious? Well, let's look at this. The term *twenty-year project* was described by Bill Clinton to Leon Panetta aboard Air Force One in 1996. Panetta asked the president why he had employed Dick Morris for so long. The president said, "You have to understand, Hillary and I have this twenty-year project. The purpose is to reshape the Democratic party and to capture the presidency."

So, in essence, even before they took their marital vows, Bill and

Hillary took their political vows. When young people are in love, they usually talk about getting married and having a home and a family. But these two were focused first on reshaping the Democratic party and capturing the presidency. And the reason why they employed Dick Morris, the president explained to Panetta, was to learn how to defeat their enemies. So that was the twenty-year project. And yes, it was audacious, and ambitious. But that's not why it's interesting.

In trying to capture the essential lack of authenticity of Hillary's candidacy, Tony Blankley has written this of her:

> In the Democratic Party race, the current leader and likely nominee, Hillary Milhous Clinton, is by prior and now private inclination an anti-military radical feminist Euro-Socialist cum Trotskyite who is masquerading as a pro-military, pro-free market, religious centrist.
>
> I think that captures the Hillary personality. Nobody can think she believes the things she's currently saying, but she's prepared to mouth them. Each time she repeats her scripted lines, she gets a few more votes. But we know her history, and we know you can't completely change your world vision at forty-five or forty-seven. You might change it at nineteen, you might change it at twenty-five, but when you've lived the better part of a political life as a Lefty, unless you have an epiphany, and she clearly has not had an epiphany, you are simply masquerading when you play the part of a political centrist.

WHAT'S IN STORE FOR THE CAMPAIGN AHEAD?

Every participant in our film (and book) believed we will be seeing the dirtiest, nastiest campaign imaginable with the Clintons seeking to destroy anybody in their way. Tony Blankley recalls how a friend of the Clintons once described them:

Their one-time friend Webb Hubbell famously said the Clintons are like a tornado that wreaks destruction on people. If you look at people who have been either close to the Clintons or opposed to them, there's truth to the notion that when the Clintons talk about being victims of the politics of personal destruction, their words are mirroring the reality.

Edward Klein agrees, having learned a thing or two about the Clinton War Room:

After writing *The Truth About Hillary*, I became an expert on the Clinton War Room. They came after me tooth and nail. I don't think any of the contenders for the presidency understand to what degree the Clintons will use the dirtiest tricks to win.

Hillary is surrounded by a group of loyal, dedicated warriors—mostly women, some men—who are battle hardened and willing to do whatever it takes to win. They see politics as war by other means. And they wage war for unconditional surrender.

I wouldn't underestimate her politically. She's tough. She's got the biggest political machine. She's got the brand name. She's got a press that's not doing as good a job as it could in unraveling the truth about her. She's got a lot of skilled advisors and slick marketers. She's got money. Put all of that together, and she's a juggernaut.

Jeff Gerth is also familiar with the Clinton War Room and sees an essential difference between the Clintons and other politicians in the way they wage political warfare:

She's different from most politicians in how she deals with criticism, whether it's from opponents, the press, or even her own staff. In that regard, she's ferocious. Going back to 1992, Hillary headed up a defense team operation that literally operated out of a bunker in Little

Rock. Her job was to suppress, cover up, intimidate, do whatever it took to keep negative information about her and Bill from becoming public. And they did a very effective job.

Despite the powerhouse organization she has put together, Bob Novak expects Hillary to run into difficulties in her campaign for the most personal of reasons:

I once got into a little trouble for writing that when Hillary was running the healthcare program, she reminded me of girls I knew in college who studied hard, knew all the answers in class, but weren't so nice. That may seem a superficial comment, but she doesn't come across as a nice person. She comes across hard, even when she's trying to smile.

Now if you go up to Capitol Hill in the Senate and House, you'll find a lot of hard people. But the presidency is different. It has been said that this is the most personal political choice that Americans make. They may elect Hillary to the Senate from New York—it's not a personal choice; it doesn't require a lot of thought. But the presidency?

When I was younger, I did a lot of door-to-door interviewing. I was always amazed at how undecided voters reacted quite personally to candidates. It was as if they were picking a wife or a husband or picking a friend. They want personality traits they can trust. And on that count, Hillary Clinton has great defects.

Defects or not, Larry Kudlow believes she's a force to be reckoned with:

I'm very impressed with her operation—and that starts at the top. Look at the debates. She clobbered Barack Obama and John Edwards. Her lead has expanded with each new debate. She's extremely well prepared. I'm impressed with that. She's got better game, and I'm impressed with that.

No successful candidate for president has ever begun a race with such high negative ratings among potential voters. But Tony Blankley cautions about reading too much into Hillary's high negatives:

> Hillary's negatives are historically high, but they are not disqualifying. Everybody's negatives are higher now than they were twenty, thirty years ago. We used to think that if you had negatives above thirty, thirty-five you were in a danger zone. Now politicians at all the levels—governor, senator, president, congress—routinely get elected with negatives in the forties because there's a general public negativity regarding all politicians.
>
> Depending on the kind of campaign the Republican candidate runs, and the kind of campaign Hillary runs, either one could win.

IS THE ELECTION HILLARY'S TO LOSE?

According to the polls, Hillary has a core base of support among women. Says Jeff Gerth:

> Despite Eleanor Roosevelt's statement in 1934 that a woman should not be elected president simply because women rally around her, that is the core reason many people think she will be elected president. And two, I would say the press has done an only adequate-at-best job of reporting on her and bringing her misstatements and her record to the public's attention. As a result, there's a lot that people don't know about her.

WHAT COULD GUARANTEE A HILLARY VICTORY?

There are personal foibles in our politicians that bear on their performance, and so, in the view of Michael Medved, they matter:

There are so many allegations about the Clintons, but only some are true. I don't believe in the Clinton Circle of Death. I don't believe these are murderous people. Having said that, the one thing that would ensure a landslide victory for Hillary, God forbid, would be Bill dying. All of a sudden, this would become a holy cause—win one for the Zipper!

Can you imagine the national convention? If something happened to Bill, they'd have a portrait the size of a football field overlooking the dais. It would be like a Leni Riefenstahl movie. Bill has had a heart attack, so it's possible.

I don't think Hillary is Lady Macbeth. I don't believe any of the wild caricatures of her. Indeed, if she were half as witchy as some people maintain, she would have figured out that her best move politically would be for something happen to Bill. And she would never do that.

Another thing that's relevant about the styles of the Clintons is the public personas they've created for themselves. Their entire persona is wrapped around concern for ordinary people. They want to raise minimum wage. They work on behalf of suffering people in Africa. They see themselves uplifting the downtrodden. And yet they don't like spending any time with the downtrodden. They like spending time with the superrich and glamorous. Bill's new best friend is Ron Burkle, a billionaire.

Is this a sign of hypocrisy?

Hillary's first political awareness was in the civil rights movement. She had previously been a Goldwater Girl from a well-to-do family in a tony Chicago suburb. She was suddenly awakened by the racism and the antiwar battles of the 1960s. The problem for Hillary is that some of that radicalism of the sixties, which we all got caught up in, devolved into anti-Americanism. People lost the sense of how fortunate we are in this country. They went out into the streets spelling America with a "k" to give it a nazi feel—Amerika. They got crazy about American imperialism.

Hillary was not immune to that.

John Kerry was not immune to it; I think it helped destroy his candidacy because he definitely drank very deeply of the anti-American Kool-aid after Vietnam. He never fully repudiated his anti-war positions convincingly.

If Hillary falls into the same trap, she won't win.

The world's greatest hatred today is not anti-Semitism; it's not homophobia or sexism or ageism. The world's greatest hatred right now is anti-Americanism. It's a poison. It ruins countries. It is every bit as irrational as racism or any other -ism. And it needs to be confronted. [Because the truth is,] this country is bursting with goodness and kindness.

| 11 |

IF YOU COULD ASK HILLARY ONE QUESTION . . .

We asked the participants in our film and book to imagine that they were sitting down with Hillary and could ask her one question. Here are the questions they would ask.

"SENATOR CLINTON . . ."

JEFF GERTH

Why at so many points in your career have you found it necessary when you've made a mistake or misjudgment to dig yourself deeper into the hole instead of just addressing the mistake and moving on?

NEWT GINGRICH

What do you really think it will take to make America secure? And would you be willing to share that with the whole country *before* you're nominated?

JOE CONNOR

Why would you release unrepentant FALN terrorists on the American people? And how could you have disrespected the memory of my father, Frank Connor, and the other victims in that way?

BILLY DALE

What did I do to justify your full-court attack on me and my family?

GARY ALDRICH

Why are you so angry?

DICK ARMEY

I'll ask what I've asked so many liberals over the years, and asked sincerely: How did you get to be that way?

BAY BUCHANAN

How can you ask the American people to make you the commander in chief when you won't take responsibility for sending our soldiers into Iraq?

DAN BURTON

Why did you feel it was necessary to mislead the American people on so many occasions?

AMANDA CARPENTER

How did you know in 2003 that the Iraq War was justified, but you don't know now? What's changed from then until now?

FRANK GAFFNEY

Are you prepared to take concrete steps to counter hostile ideologies and to defeat the states that are enabling them?

EDWARD KLEIN
Given all the people you have damaged and destroyed, has it all been worth it?

LARRY KUDLOW
Is there any way I can persuade you that tax simplification and lower tax rates would be good for the economy, good for growth, and good for every single American?

RICK HAHN
How can the American public trust you on decisions dealing with terrorism without thinking you might first consider your own political agenda?

LEE HIEB
Have you ever come out of your ivory tower and really talked to people in Canada, Mexico, and these other countries that have socialized healthcare?

CLARE LOPEZ
How will you deal with a broad-based international movement bent on destroying liberal democracy?

BOB NOVAK
I know she wouldn't answer any question I put to her. But if I were using some kind of truth drug, I'd ask, "Hillary, what would your model for government be?"

ANGELA McGLOWAN
Is this some goal you decided in first grade you wanted to do, some dream of yours; is it anything more than that?

RICHARD MINITER

Is there anything that you believed was true and right in 1968, which you now believe is wrong or wrongheaded?

KATHLEEN WILLEY

How can you stand before us all as an advocate of women and expect us to think that you should be elected the first [woman] president of [the] United States after the role that you have played in the ruination of so many women?

JARED STERN

Do you ever think about the damage you've done to these women—do you ever think about them?

DICK MORRIS

If we elect you president, will you try to push your old healthcare program through again?

KATE O'BEIRNE

Was the unpleasantness you endured in the '90s the result of a vast right-wing conspiracy or the result of your husband's reckless juvenile appetites?

MICHAEL MEDVED

After all you've been through, was it worth it?

BUZZ PATTERSON

Do you really believe this nation needs you?

TONY BLANKLEY

A lot of people would love to ask Hillary one question before the election.

Having dealt with the Clintons for years, I know that truth is not likely to be the product of their utterances, so I would never ask her any questions. I wouldn't believe any answer.

SPECIAL APPENDIX

(A NEW LOOK AT A CASE WORTH REVISITING)

BACK TO THE FUTURES:
HILLARY CLINTON'S CATTLE TRADES REVEAL CUT CORNERS,
STUFFED POCKETS, AND CASH FOR FAVORS

By Deroy Murdock

NEW YORK — As Hillary Clinton continues her long march toward the Democratic nomination, old expressions like "Whitewater," "Rose Law Firm," and "missing billing records" surely will resurface. Another such phrase is "cattle futures." It triggers colorful images of rugged cowboys rustling steers and branding bulls. A more accurate picture, however, involves slick securities traders cutting corners and peddling influence.

Hillary Clinton's ten-month foray in this field generated sky-high profits that remain as pungent as a mountain of manure. Her adventures in the arcane, volatile world of cattle-futures trading include fishy transactions, scheming corporate lawyers, morally challenged commodities brokers, and a hefty jackpot for her and her husband, Arkansas's then attorney general and subsequent governor, William Jefferson Clinton. The Clintons' bonanza parallels the payout in public favors that Tyson Foods, Inc.—Arkansas's largest employer and America's premier poultry company—enjoyed once Hillary cashed in her cattle contracts.

Even twenty-eight years hence, these odd deals serve as windows onto the Clintonian ethical landscape. The view isn't pretty.

On April 3, 1994, as this story erupted among the countless controversies that characterized the Clinton years, the Memphis *Commercial Appeal*'s Ted Evanoff explained how this system works. A live cattle-futures contract is a commitment to purchase or deliver twenty tons of beef, at a date and price stated in each contract. These agreements help ranchers and butchers predict prices and plan accordingly. A typical trader aims to sell such a contract to a slaughterhouse before its delivery date. Otherwise, a tractor trailer will drive up to his office lobby, while about thirty-eight bovines wait to be sent up to, say, the thirty-fifth floor conference room to await further instructions.

Hillary Clinton entered this business beside James Blair. He was external counsel, and later general counsel, to Tyson Foods. Blair served as Clinton's advisor and tour guide through the cattle-futures labyrinth. In fact, he apparently took a rather hands-on approach to Clinton's portfolio. "I think it's become clear he placed most of the trades," then White House spokeswoman Dee Dee Myers admitted in April 1994.

Hillary Clinton invested where Blair and Tyson did their bidding—with the Springdale, Arkansas, office of Chicago-based Ray E. Friedman & Co. (REFCO). Clinton's dealer was a World Series of Poker semifinalist and thirteen-year Tyson Foods alumnus fittingly named Robert L. "Red" Bone. Shortly before working with Clinton, James Ring Adams reported in the August 1994 *American Spectator*, Red Bone "had completed a one-year partial suspension on charges of plotting to manipulate the egg-futures market on the Chicago Mercantile Exchange. (He later received a second, more serious suspension for violating the first one.)"

According to the *Commercial Appeal*'s Evanoff, investors in the late 1970s could purchase single contracts for about $700 in margin money. And into this cattle casino Hillary Clinton hoofed.

Clinton's maiden trade on October 11, 1978, was a purchase of ten contracts worth $12,000, even though she had just $1,000 in her account. By day's end she had made $5,300, a nifty, 530 percent profit. Perhaps she was blessed with good fortune. Or maybe she learned plenty from reading the *Wall Street Journal*, to which she attributed much of her trading prowess.

Experts consider this an unusually large turnover for such a trading position in just one session. A $2,840 profit seems to be the maximum one normally could have made under those circumstances.

So, after just one day in her new career as a cattle-futures trader, questions already began to swirl like flies around Hillary Clinton.

"What has made analysts wonder about her venture is the initial transaction," Evanoff wrote. "She reported not $2,840 in profits on her first deal, but $5,300. And analysts wonder whether she or someone else was directing her trading activity."

"Even if she had been clever enough to buy at the very bottom and sell at the very top, it would have taken more than one contract for her to make that kind of money," the Futures Industries Association's John M. Damgard told Evanoff.

Hillary Clinton's trades coincided with REFCO's habit of buying cattle contracts en masse, then later allocating wins and losses among clients, often independently of how they actually invested. This is a bit like handing out a tavern's bar tabs to patrons after last call—not according to actual booze intake, but by giving the low-cost checks to favored guests, and the big tickets to poorly regarded suckers. Alternatively, some clients could absorb losing trades in order to enrich other account holders by having REFCO give them winning hands that they really hadn't earned.

This practice came alive on June 27, 1979. According to Chicago Mercantile Exchange records obtained by the *Wall Street Journal*, Red Bone and a colleague exceeded their trading limits that day. Normally, traders are allowed three hundred contracts each, daily. That June 27, these two brokers sold "short" 1,443 feeder-cattle contracts.

But that's not all.

As *USA Today* reported on April 25, 1994, Bill McCurdy and Steven Johns, two REFCO brokers in Springdale, testified in an investor's fraud lawsuit against REFCO. As court records reveal, McCurdy and Johns swore that they covered up block trading one summer afternoon. They said they were directed to lock themselves in their offices after the market closed, turn back the clocks used to time-stamp trading slips, and then create bogus, individual customer-trading orders that could be substituted for that day's actual, massive block orders. Asked in one legal case if he considered such block trading proper, McCurdy answered: "I don't think that it is."

And just when was this flurry of impropriety? June 27, 1979.

That happened to be the day when Hillary Clinton invested in fifty cattle-futures contracts. "It was Clinton's biggest single trade with REFCO, and the most profitable," Kevin Johnson and Bill Montague reported in the April 7, 1994, *USA Today*. She cleared $43,760 that day. June 27, 1979, also is one of just three days whose trading records the Clinton White House says were lost.

Such enormous volume required a margin deposit of $60,000. However, trading records indicate that Clinton had just $25,011 in her account. That July 12, Clinton carried a $41,740 loss in one trade, $22,155 in a second, and a $2,625 profit in a third. REFCO rules called for Clinton to deposit $92,364 in her account to underwrite such exposure. Woulda, shoulda, coulda. That didn't happen.

As Charles Babcock observed in the May 27, 1994, *Washington Post*, "Although Hillary Rodham Clinton's account was under-margined for nearly all of July 1979, no margin calls were made, no additional cash was put up, and she eventually reaped a $60,000 profit."

While this smacked of favoritism, then White House aide John Podesta disagreed: "We don't believe Mrs. Clinton got different treatment than other REFCO clients."

Stanley Greenwood might beg to differ. That July 12, Hillary Clinton avoided a margin call that abruptly would have made her cows come home. Greenwood, who also traded with REFCO's Springdale office, saw his investments liquidated when he did not deposit $48,000 against his losses.

In a lawsuit filed against Red Bone, REFCO client Randall Barnes said he covered his trading losses in 1978 by handing Bone the mortgage to his farm.

Clinton's final trades were "a confusing flourish," James Ring Adams wrote. Before throwing in her lasso, she traded separate blocks of fifty contracts. Seemingly carrying both long and short positions, she bet cattle prices would go both up *and* down. Perhaps with her head spinning, Hillary Clinton dismounted this bucking bronco on July 23, 1979. She finally closed her REFCO account in October 1979, just before cattle prices plunged, impoverishing many of her fellow cattle speculators. She never saddled up again.

So what if Hillary Clinton and her husband benefited from irregular trades twenty-eight years ago? Shouldn't this be brisket under the bridge? If their business were kosher, certainly so. But these trades reek of favoritism at best and fraud at worst. If Hillary Clinton, then Arkansas's first lady, received special handling, was anything expected in return?

It seems significant that Clinton prospered under the guidance of Tyson's lawyer, James Blair. "I trusted Jim Blair and it worked for me," she once said.

In 1978 and 1979, Tyson Foods also was a major client at REFCO's Springdale office, where it maintained three corporate accounts. Still hazy after all these years is whether this haystack of excessive and back-dated trading slips let REFCO pitchfork losses into Tyson's accounts and gains into Clinton's portfolio.

"The directing of a huge bundle of money into the Clinton pocket," syndicated columnist William Safire wrote in 1994, "could be classified under a word that has only been whispered in connection with this deal: bribery, in its most modern form."

As Bill Clinton's governorship unfolded, Tyson received at least $9 million in Arkansas State loans. Meanwhile, environmental regulators in Little Rock also tread lightly on Tyson, allowing it to pour chicken waste into local rivers.

Tyson Foods "would continue during the Clinton years in Little Rock to be one of the most powerful forces in Arkansas," Roger Morris wrote in *Partners in Power: The Clintons and Their America* (Henry Holt, 1995). Tyson benefited from "tens of millions in state-promoted business and literally billions in ongoing income derived under a regime of regulatory, tax, and other political advantages."

Tyson Foods also had a special place at the table during the Clinton presidency. In spring 1994, the U.S. Department of Agriculture blocked a bid to extend to poultry a "zero tolerance" standard for fecal matter that applied to other meats. As Wilson Horne, USDA's former chief meat inspector told the Associated Press: "The message was very, very loud and clear that we were to stop the process."

In what was nicknamed the "Chechens for Chickens Affair," President Clinton backed Russian president Boris Yeltsin's reelection bid in 1995, despite Moscow's belligerent response to the Chechen independence movement. In exchange, summit notes revealed, Yeltsin lifted a Russian ban on American chicken, a very convenient trade concession for Tyson.

In August 1997, former agriculture secretary Mike Espy was indicted for corruption amid charges that Tyson tried to influence him with illegal gratuities. On December 2, 1998, Espy was acquitted on all thirty counts in his federal indictment. In a plea agreement with special prosecutor Donald Smaltz, Tyson Foods admitted to attempting to influence Espy with $12,000 in sports tickets, airplane travel, meals, and other gifts. Tyson even gave Espy's girlfriend, Patricia Dempsey, a $1,200 college scholarship. It paid $4 million in fines and $2 million in investigative costs for trying to make friends in high places.

As the Clintons loaded up their moving van with White House antiques in December 2000, President Clinton pardoned virtually everyone whom Smaltz prosecuted.

"Even the people who pleaded guilty got a pardon," said William Jeffress, attorney for Tyson executive Archie Schaffer III. As the Associated Press reported, Schaffer was convicted in 1998 of trying to sway Espy illegally by inviting him to a party for Tyson chief Don "Big Daddy" Tyson. "Every warm human being got relief," during Clinton's pardon-o-rama, Jeffress said.

Others in this cattle caper found themselves in legal trouble:

In late 1979, the Chicago Mercantile Exchange disciplined REFCO for "serious and repeated violations of record-keeping functions, order-entry procedures, margin requirements, and hedge procedures," according to Merc records obtained by the *Wall Street Journal.* The Merc fined REFCO $250,000 (back then, its largest penalty ever), suspended Red Bone for three years, and disciplined several of his associates.

Federal juries in Arkansas convicted REFCO of defrauding customers and brokers by trying to manipulate the cattle-futures market. However, these verdicts eventually were overturned on appeal.

So what did the Clintons get for this cyclone of sleaze that spun around them?

"During the period she was trading commodities, she and her husband owned no substantial assets and were living on a combined income of about $50,000 a year," Sara Fritz and John Broder reported in the April 5, 1994, *Los Angeles Times*.

In the end, Hillary Clinton's $1,000 bet yielded $99,540, a return on investment of roughly 10,000 percent, far beyond the 1,700 percent gain the *American Spectator*'s James Ring Adams believes an investor legitimately could have garnered during this period. Researchers at Auburn University and the University of North Florida in 1995 compared Hillary Clinton's futures records with market data from the *Wall Street Journal* at the time she traded. As they reported in the *Journal of Economics and Statistics*, their computer model calculated that the probability that her profits were legitimate was less than one in 250 million.

The Clintons reportedly used these astronomical earnings for a down payment on a home, plus some tax-free municipal bonds. While this is no small sum today, the Bureau of Labor Statistics' Inflation Calculator indicates that $100,000 in 1979 would equal $287,790.63 in 2007. Not bad. Not bad at all.

Martin Elgison, an Atlanta attorney who represented a lawyer who lost money trading at REFCO, said this about Hillary Clinton's cattle trades: "One can speculate it was just luck, or it was something more sinister."

New York commentator Deroy Murdock is a columnist with the Scripps Howard News Service and a media fellow with the Hoover Institution on War, Revolution and Peace at Stanford University.

ABOUT CITIZENS UNITED

Citizens United is an organization dedicated to restoring our government to citizens' control. Through a combination of education, advocacy, and grassroots organization, Citizens United seeks to reassert the traditional American values of limited government, freedom of enterprise, strong families, and national sovereignty and security. Citizens United's goal is to restore the founding fathers' vision of a free nation, guided by the honesty, common sense, and goodwill of its citizens.

Just as the pamphlet was the persuasive tool of choice to colonists such as Thomas Paine, we believe the documentary film has become a vital part of the great political conversation we have in this country. Citizens United completed six films by the end of 2007, and four are available for purchase at this time.

Go to this Web site and "Visit Our Store"
www.citizensunited.org

Other Movies from Citizen United

Border War—The Battle over Illegal Immigration

The human and drug trafficking across the border with Mexico is nothing short of an *invasion*. As dangers and concerns escalate on both sides, *Border War* documents the lives of five individuals affected directly by the immigration invasion. Prepare for an entirely new outlook on this escalating crisis.

Broken Promises—The UN at 60

From its silence on hostilities between India and Pakistan in 1947, the Arab/Israeli conflicts of the late 1940s, Pol Pot's slaughter of millions of Cambodian refugees in the 1970s, genocides in Rwanda and Bosnia, the present-day oil for food scandal—has the UN lived up to its charter? Can the UN ever be made to work?

ACLU—At War With America

Under the guise of protecting the civil liberties of ordinary citizens, the ACLU has become the mouthpiece and legal bloodhound for left-wing fringe groups—many of which actively seek to undermine the very foundations of our great democracy. Here we unmask their true motives and offer viewers an opportunity to take back their precious liberties!

Celsius 41.11—The Truth Behind the Lies of *Fahrenheit 9/11*

Never before had one film so deceived voters, and Michael Moore was laughing all the way to the bank. Into the political breach stepped *Celsius 41.11* to expose the sleight of film Moore used to distort the truth. This is the film that started the intelligent conservative response to the nutcase liberal lie.

Citizens United

1006 Pennsylvania Ave. SE • Washington, D.C. 20003 • (202) 547-5420